The Problem of Forming Social Capital

Political Evolution and Institutional Change
Bo Rothstein and Sven Steinmo, editors

Exploring the dynamic relationships among political institutions, attitudes, behaviors, and outcomes, this series is problem-driven and pluralistic in methodology. It examines the evolution of governance, public policy, and political economy in different national and historical contexts.

It will explore social dilemmas, such as collective-action problems, and enhance understanding of how political outcomes result from the interaction among political ideas—including values, beliefs, or social norms—institutions, and interests. It will promote cutting-edge work in historical institutionalism, rational choice, and game theory, and the processes of institutional change and/or evolutionary models of political history.

Restructuring the Welfare State: Political Institutions and Policy Change
Edited by Bo Rothstein and Sven Steinmo

The Problem of Forming Social Capital: Why Trust?
By Francisco Herreros

The Personal and the Political: How Personal Welfare State Experiences Affect Political Trust and Ideology
By Staffan Kumlin

Building a Trustworthy State in Post-Socialist Transition
Edited by János Kornai and Susan Rose-Ackerman

Creating Social Trust in Post-Socialist Transition
Edited by János Kornai, Bo Rothstein, and Susan Rose-Ackerman

The Problem of Forming Social Capital: Why Trust?

Francisco Herreros

THE PROBLEM OF FORMING SOCIAL CAPITAL : WHY TRUST?
© Francisco Herreros, 2004

First published 2004 by
PALGRAVE MACMILLAN™
175 Fifth Avenue, New York, N.Y. 10010 and
Houndmills, Basingstoke, Hampshire, England RG21 6XS
Companies and representatives throughout the world

PALGRAVE MACMILLAN is the global academic imprint of the Palgrave Macmillan division of St. Martin's Press, LLC and of Palgrave Macmillan Ltd. Macmillan® is a registered trademark in the United States, United Kingdom and other countries. Palgrave is a registered trademark in the European Union and other countries.

ISBN 1–4039–6482–3 hardback

Library of Congress Cataloging-in-Publication Data
Herreros, Francisco
    The problem of forming social capital : why trust? / by Francisco Herreros.
        p. cm.—(Political evolution and institutional change)
    Includes bibliographical references
    ISBN 1–4039–6482–3
    1. Social capital (Sociology) I. Title. II. Series.

HM708.V39 2004
302—dc22   2003060870

A catalogue record for this book is available from the British Library.

Design by Newgen Imaging Systems (P) Ltd., Chennai, India.

First edition: June 2004

10 9 8 7 6 5 4 3 2 1

Printed in the United States of America.

CONTENTS

ACKNOWLEDGMENTS

The first person I wish to thank is José María Maravall, who read all the chapters of the book from the first drafts. He was very distrustful about social capital from the beginning, but fortunately he did not distrust my capacity to carry on with this project. His distrust had beneficial effects, perhaps not for the wider community, as social trust has, but for the quality of the book. I had to refine my arguments as much as I could to obtain his approval.

Second, I would like to thank to the *Centro de Estudios Avanzados en Ciencias Sociales* of the *Instituto Juan March*, in Madrid. I was granted with a research scholarship in this institution in 1996. In the Juan March Institute I began my studies about social capital, and much more than that, I evolved as a social scientist. The Juan March Institute is a wonderful place for research and training in sociology and political science. This book is to a great extent the outcome of the support and the incentives offered by the *Instituto Juan March*.

For discussion of various arguments and chapters of the book, I owe special thanks to Henar Criado. Actually, thanks to Henar the book has been considerably improved since its first version. She has helped me to further clarify my arguments, to add new ones, and she has supported me along the entire process of writing this book. I also thank Andrés de Francisco (who spoke to me first about social capital in 1996), Carles Boix (who read a previous version of some of the chapters), Steven Rosenstone (who gave me good advice regarding the preliminary project of the book when he was a member of the scientific committee of the Juan March Institute) and Justin Byrne, that helped me with the English version of the book. Margaret Levi read the entire book and made many intelligent comments on it, both written and in the conversations we had when she was in Madrid. She has helped a lot to develop my arguments, and I owe her, more than anybody, many thanks for her invaluable and generous help in publishing the manuscript.

Part of the writing of the book was carried out while I was a researcher in the IESAA/CSIC. I wish to thank the IESAA for its support. I specially thank Fernando Aguiar for his comments on various chapters of the book.

Parts of this work were presented in various workshops in the European Consortium for Political Research Joint Sessions: the workshop on democratic innovation directed by Michael Saward in Manheim (1999), the workshop on voluntary associations and democracy directed by Sigrid Rossteutcher in Torino (2001), and the workshop on republicanism directed Iseult Honahan and Jeremy Jennings in Edinburgh (2003). I thank the organizers and the participants in these workshops for their comments. I specially wish to thank the comments by Dietlind Stolle in the Torino workshop.

Finally, I dedicate this book to Henar and to my parents Francisco and Josefina.

Finally, I wish to thank David Pervin and Melissa Nosal at Palgrave Publishers for their help in editing the book.

CHAPTER ONE

Introduction

Over the last two decades, the literature on social capital has grown to a point where its contribution is worth evaluating. At first glance, this certainly appears to have been a very fertile line of research. Although social capital is not yet considered a form of capital on equal terms with human and physical capital, its place in sociological and political science literature is assured. However, social capital literature is flawed by, among other things, the use of inadequate definitions and the debatable conclusions drawn with respect to its relations with other variables.

In this work I deal directly and indirectly with some of the defects of the social capital research paradigm. In order for social capital to be considered a third form of capital, we should be able to answer the following questions: What is social capital? How can we invest in social capital? What have been the effects of this form of capital to date? The research into social capital has been especially productive in answering the third question, silent with regard to the second, and vague and verbose with regard to the first. In the following chapters, I focus above all on the second question. However, research into the sources of social capital requires, first, a definition. Hence, although this is not my main proposition, I also propose an answer to this first question, that is, the definition of social capital.

In fact, at first sight the third question—the effects of social capital on other variables—would appear to offer the most promising line of research. It is hardly surprising, therefore, that this has attracted most interest to date. Social capital is interesting precisely because of its supposed effects on other variables. For example, it is said that social capital is a key factor in the reduction of the transaction costs associated with economic exchanges, and thus, is considered an important factor for economic development.

However, the success of the social capital paradigm is more probably due to its supposedly beneficial effects for democracy. It is assumed that higher stocks of social capital are synonymous with better-working democracies, in which citizens are more active and demand greater accountability from their elected representatives. Although these effects have yet to be demonstrated conclusively, there is some evidence to support this thesis. If this is indeed correct, the question I am trying to answer—what is social capital and how can we create it?—would also be of importance for improving the functioning of democracy. Some of my proposals are radically different from those put forward in much of the social capital literature. In particular, the traditional social capital research paradigm has generally held that the development of civil society is hampered by the excessive presence of the State. The State has been considered, at very best, irrelevant for the creation of social capital. In contrast, I argue that the State can play an important role in generating social capital, especially by facilitating participation in democratic organizations, that, in turn, I suggest plays a particularly important role in the creation of social capital.

Many readers would surely ask: why another book on social capital? Given the accumulation of works on this topic in the last few years, this is not an irrelevant question. A good answer to this question, one that attracts the readers' interest in the book, has to rely on one assumption: social capital is a useful resource for society. As I have said, the consequences of social capital on the wider society is the privileged topic in the social capital research agenda. I do not deal with this topic in this book. But if you think that social capital is important, say, for democracy or economic development (and the evidence about this I think is, at least, promising), you will be interested in a book that tries to explain why some communities are blessed with higher levels of social capital than others, and what can be done to overcome these differences in social capital. My main contention in this book is that if we depart with low levels of social capital, we are not condemned to a vicious circle of low social capital, low economic growth, governmental inefficiency, lower social capital, and so on. We can put in motion virtuous circles of the creation of social capital.

To conclude this introduction, and before providing a definition of social capital, I would like to say something about my methodological approach. In order to answer the two questions posed in this study, I draw extensively on the tools of rational choice theory. In particular, in chapters 4 and 5 I use game theory to illustrate various explanatory mechanisms relating mainly to the creation of social capital. This reference to the methodological approach to the study of social capital is by no means irrelevant given that social capital has been presented, notably by Coleman (1988) and Taylor (1996), as a useful analytical tool for minimizing the limitations of rational choice theory, or to use Coleman's words, as a way of bridging the gap between the "under" and "super" socialized conceptions of the human being used, respectively, by economists and sociologists. In fact, I have very little to say in this study about this debate. Nevertheless, my approach to key concepts in the social capital literature, such as trust, cannot be fully identified with either/any of these approaches. On the one hand, it differs somewhat from the standard assumptions of the strict theory of rationality, while, on the other, it is not identified with what Sztompka (1999), for example, considers a sociological analysis of trust. Expectations of trust are not always rational, at least in terms of the criteria of the strict theory of rationality. For example, I assume that individuals are boundedly rational in their decisions, through a combination of limited computational capacity and the complexity of their environment. Thus, I follow the assumption of bounded rationality adopted by transaction cost economics. Additionally, I assume that the beliefs people have, for example, about other people, are not always strictly rational. People often use rules to deal with uncertainty in the formation of beliefs that have little to do with probability theory. In other cases, these beliefs are not even consistent with the available information. Their preferences are also heterogeneous. That is, they do not only have egoistic preferences, as is assumed in most rational choice models, but can also be altruistic, conditional cooperators, or kantians. This does not mean that their decisions and beliefs are irrational. Nonselfish preferences are easily introduced in rational choice theory. Altruistic preferences mean simply that you include another person's utility as an argument in your utility function. Moreover, although people in some cases have limited information, far from perfect computational capacity, and poorly founded beliefs, decisions to cooperate can be explained in terms of benefits, expectations, and potential costs. It is debatable whether people's expectations are irrational when they are not entirely well founded, that is, when the individual does not collate all the relevant information. When I give examples of individuals using some type of shortcut to form expectations, I do not judge the rationality of those expectations. In accordance with Popkin (1991), I consider that such expectations are not necessarily irrational, provided that the individual reaches the same conclusions she would have done if she had collated all the relevant information.

In this book I begin by defining the term "social capital." Surprisingly perhaps, I do not assume that trust and voluntary associations in themselves constitute social capital. Even though social networks and the relations of trust derived from them are crucial elements in a definition of social capital, I consider social capital to be formed exclusively by obligations of reciprocity, derived in most cases from relations of trust, and by the information potential offered by social networks. In chapter 3, I discuss the problem of social capital formation. It is widely recognized that the creation of social capital is problematic because social capital has certain characteristics in common with a public good. The usual solution to this problem is to see its creation as a by-product of other activities. In this light, I try and answer the question of how we can explain the differences in social capital between communities. In order to do so, I go beyond explanations founded on the creation of social capital as a by-product. In chapters 4–6, I develop the central arguments of my research by analyzing the creation of social capital. Even though I refer to the ways in which social networks generate information for their members, these chapters focus on the question of the creation of trust. The reason is that the generation of information as a by-product of participation in social networks is a relatively noncontroversial issue, whereas the creation of trust, especially social trust, is a much more complex process. In each chapter, I empirically test the theoretical hypothesis. This empirical testing combines quantitative analysis, using logistic, multilevel and simultaneous equation models, with a more qualitative analysis of historical cases. It should be noted, however, that these historical cases are not used to test my hypotheses, but merely to illustrate them.

CHAPTER TWO

The Concept of Social Capital

Social capital is a concept that has only recently been incorporated into the social sciences. Two decades ago there were hardly any references to this unusual form of capital, although some almost archeological research has dated the first appearance of the concept to a book written in 1916 by the American reformist L. J. Hanifan (Putnam, 2000: 19).[1] The last 20 years, however, have witnessed a boom in studies of social capital. Economists, sociologists, and especially, political scientists, have embraced the concept enthusiastically. The result is a dense body of literature that uses social capital as an independent variable to explain a series of phenomena ranging from the creation of human capital and the effectiveness of democratic institutions to the reduction of crime or the eradication of poverty.

What, however, is social capital? Twenty years of research might be thought to be enough for the emergence of an agreed definition of this form of capital. Yet, this is not in fact the case. One definition maintains that social capital is a form of capital akin to human and physical capital, which it is possible to invest in and deploy in order to attain certain ends. Another approach suggests that it consists of certain individual values (like, e.g., civic virtue) that have, fortunately, beneficial consequences for the rest of the community. In this chapter I outline the definition of social capital that I use throughout this book. This definition is closer to that developed by James Coleman than those employed by most political scientists.

According to James Coleman, the term social capital was first used by Glenn Loury (1977) to refer to the resources inherent in family relations, which are drawn upon in the cognitive development of the child. However, further research shows that the concept of social capital and its current influence in the social sciences can largely be attributed to Pierre Bourdieu (1985), James Coleman (1988, 1990), and Robert Putnam (1993a, 2000).

The structural definition of social capital is mainly derived from the work of Bourdieu and Coleman, both of whom define social capital as a range of resources available to individuals thanks to their participation in social networks. More specifically, Bourdieu (1985: 248) defines social capital as the "aggregate of real or potential resources that are associated to the possession of a durable network of more or less institutionalized relations of mutual recognition." According to Coleman (1990: 103), two key features characterize social capital: it consists of some aspect of the social structure, and it facilitates certain actions by individuals who are situated within this structure. Resources derived from participation in social networks can include, for example, the acquisition of information, obligations of reciprocity derived from systems of mutual trust,[2] or the use of cooperative social norms. In any event, it is important to stress that these authors consider that the access of individuals to resources of social capital depends on their participation in some form of social relation (Foley and Edwards, 1999: 166).

Social capital, therefore, is a resource which, like human and physical capital, makes it easier to achieve certain ends. Moreover, it shares with human capital its intangibility, although this characteristic is probably more pronounced in the case of social capital. It is this intangibility that makes it particularly difficult to identify social capital as a resource. To make this task easier, we can imagine two individuals. One lives in a Hobbesian state of nature, whereas the other is an inhabitant of a Rousseaunian world.[3] The unpleasant side of living in a Hobbesian state of nature is largely due to the absence of social capital: individuals are isolated, so are unlikely to develop relations of trust with other inhabitants of the state of nature. This prevents them from accessing information about, for example, new farming techniques developed by their neighbors. They are also unable to help their neighbors reap their harvest in the expectation that this favor will be reciprocated. They lack the resources (obligations of reciprocity and information) that might make their lives easier. It is this absence of social capital that makes it necessary to establish property rights, enforced by the State. In contrast, in Rousseau's state of nature, life is sweeter thanks to the existence of reserves of social capital. In both cases, the origin of the social capital resources does not lie in individual attitudes or values, but in networks of relations: the difference between the two states of nature is that in the Hobbesian one the individual is isolated, and, as a consequence, lacks social capital, whereas in the

Rousseaunian state the individual is not isolated, and therefore enjoys resources of social capital. It is membership of social networks that determines the individual's potential stock of social capital (Sandefur and Laumann, 1998: 484).

In the above example, I have mentioned two resources in the hands of individuals who survive as best they can in the state of nature: obligations of reciprocity associated with a relation of trust and information derived from social relations.

Even though it is a potential source of social capital, a social relation does not in itself constitute social capital. My argument here is that social capital consists simply of certain resources derived from participation in social networks. It is this participation that provides access to resources of social capital in the form of obligations of reciprocity that spring from relations of trust and of private information in the hands of other members of the social network. Social capital, then, is not trust or networks but the obligation of reciprocity that can be derived from relations of trust and the information that can be derived from the participation in social networks. From this definition it is derived that, although the analysis of trust is crucial for the social capital research agenda, trust is not in itself social capital. I now analyze these two forms of social capital, beginning with the one highlighted in most of the literature, namely the obligations of reciprocity derived from relations of trust. I then briefly analyze the information that comes from participating in social networks.

Trust and Obligations of Reciprocity

Trust is an extremely abstract concept, a factor that makes it particularly difficult to study in theoretical terms. In order to approach the concept of trust, and its nature as social capital, I begin not with trust itself, but with what is often known as the "decision to trust" (Coleman, 1990). Approached in this way, the decision to trust is associated with risks. That is, the individual faced by the decision to trust or not cannot be sure of the trustworthiness of the other party. Nevertheless, although she does not know the objective probabilities of the other individual's trustworthiness, she can form subjective expectations about it. If p is the probability of the second individual's trustworthiness, G the potential gains if the second person decides to honor the trust placed in her, and C the potential costs if she does not honor that trust (and bearing in mind that if she decides not to trust the outcome will be the *status quo ante*) the first player will decide to trust if $pG + (1 - p)C > 0$, that is, when $p/(1 - p) > C/G$ (Coleman, 1990: 99).

Thus defined, the decision to trust is a rational one. However, not everybody, would agree with this definition. In fact, most of the analysts who use trust as a, if not the, form of social capital, would reject the idea that it is exclusively or mainly a rational decision. These analysis include, for example, those who consider trust as a favorable behavior toward society (Uslaner, 1999a: 123), or as "altruistic trust": trust on behalf of others and on behalf of the wider community (Mansbridge, 1999; Putnam, 2000: 135).

Nonetheless, the equation given above incorporates a decision to trust, or, more accurately, the decision to entrust something to another person (Hardin, 2001, 2002). It is not trust itself. Trust is reflected in the expectation about the other individual's trustworthiness (p). Trust, there-fore, is a more or less well-grounded expectation about the preferences of other people. This means that the decision to entrust does not depend on trust alone. Even if we think that the probability of someone being trustworthy is very low, that is, although we do not trust them very much, we can, nevertheless, take a risk if the potential gains if they are trustworthy are much higher than the potential losses if they are not trustworthy. In this sense, it is difficult to understand trust as a means to overcome "social uncertainty," that is, the risk of being exploited in social interactions (Yamagishi et al., 1998: 170), or, in other sense, to reduce "complexity" (Luhman, 1979: 8), or to reduce the special risks inherent to modern society (Seligman, 1997: 8). You cannot decide, simply, to trust in strangers in order to overcome social uncertainty (Hardin, 2002: 10). In fact, if you trust it is because you think that the other people are trustworthy, and, thus you do not face much social uncertainty. But if you face social uncertainty, you cannot decide to trust in order to over-come this uncertainty. Notice that the definition of trust as a way to overcome uncertainty entails a sort of trade-off between trust and infor-mation. More information means less trust, because citizens do not need to trust in order to overcome uncertainty. On the contrary, less infor-mation leads to more trust, because individuals have to rely on trust to interact with unknown people. On the contrary, if we understand trust as an expectation, this trade-off between information and trust is to a great extent misleading. If you have lots of information about a given person, especially about her preferences, you could trust her or not, depending on the content of the information you have. You will trust her if this amount of information indicates that she is trustworthy. If you know, on the contrary, that she is a thief in her leisure time, you will probably not trust her if she asks you for a loan. Now imagine that you do not have any information about this person, and she asks you to do her a favor (to lend her, say, a hundred euros). You evidently face social uncertainty, because you do not know for certain if she will repay you or not. But you cannot reduce this social uncertainty by simply deciding to trust her. If you trust her (whatever the reason you have to be trustful: e.g., because your religion teaches you that all people are trustworthy), then you will probably lend her the money, but if you do not trust her, you simply cannot decide to trust. You may nonetheless give her the money because you do not care about money, or because you are a millionaire and this is your good action for the day, but the point is that your lack of information about her preferences is not translated into higher levels of trust in order to reduce social uncertainty.

Trust is, then, an expectation, not a decision. In what sense does trust constitute social capital? This is often treated as a relatively straightforward issue in the social capital literature. It is commonly assumed that trust is a form of social capital. This is an erroneous assumption, however. As I attempt to demonstrate in this chapter, trust cannot be considered per se as a form of social capital. As I have already said, social capital is obligations of reciprocity and information, both derived from membership of social networks. However, although I do not think that trust can be claimed as a form of social capital, it can play an intermediary role between membership of social networks and the generation of social capital. Membership to social networks, as voluntary associations, for example, generates relations based on trust. This means that if you cooperate with a comember of your association, this cooperation is based to a great extent in your trustful expectation about the probability that your comember will reciprocate your cooperative behavior. If the trust you place in your comember generates in him an obligation to be trustworthy, that is, to reciprocate your cooperative overture, then your trust can be claimed as a crucial element between the membership of a social network and the generation of social capital (in this case, the generation of an obligation of reciprocity by the trusted person).

As I argue in the following chapters when discussing the problem of the formation of social capital, subjective expectations about other people's trustworthiness can come from various sources, but most of them are related to the social networks to which the individual belongs. Information about people who are members of my network can help me to calculate those subjective probabilities. Another type of expectation of trust, that is, expectations with regard to unknown people, are also formed through mechanisms relating to membership of a social network. These are analyzed in chapter 5.

Although participation in social networks can be an important source of trust, as I have already said, this in itself does not mean that trust is social capital. I have already argued that social capital is a resource that facilitated the attainment of certain ends. In what sense can particular expectations about another person's behavior be considered a resource for the attainment of certain preferences? In general, and as noted earlier, this question has scarcely been addressed in the social capital literature: it is simply assumed that trust (however defined) is a form of social capital. In this section I use two arguments to prove that trust can provide resources of social capital. The first suggests that benevolent behavior toward another person will be rewarded by similar behavior on the part of that person (i.e., trust generates obligations of reciprocity). The second suggests that social trust is a resource for the trustee.

In principle, the decision to cooperate with somebody based on a positive expectation about this person's trustworthiness does not necessarily imply the expectation that this decision will be rewarded in the future by a similar decision by the trustee. Although some authors consider that trust is based on the assumption that good behavior will be repaid in the future (Newton, 1999b: 171), this is not necessarily so. The potential gains (G) that are part of the calculus of the expected utility of a decision to cooperate do not necessarily include such future benefits: the decision to cooperate can simply be based on an evaluation of current benefits. Consider, for example, the benefits derived from leaving a valuable object in someone else's care, and that object being returned to us intact. In this case, we probably do not expect that the trustee, moved by our trust in her, will consider that it is her obligation to do us a similar favor in the future. But, in this case, trust would not generate a resource of social capital, as no obligations of reciprocity are associated with the act of trust. Trust can constitute social capital if we assume that the trustee may be a creditor of a future obligation to the person giving the trust, or, in another example, if we think that our trusting behavior generates in the trustee an obligation to honor that trust.

The first condition is relatively easy to meet. It simply assumes that doing a favor permits one to ask for the favor to be returned in the future. Returning a favor can be a rational decision under certain circumstances. For example, if there is an interest in sustaining a reputation about one's trustworthiness. If you think that in the future you may need a favor from that person, then it is in your interest to maintain the impression that you are trustworthy. In Hardin's sense, this is trust as "encapsulated interest": I trust you because I expect that my interest encapsulate yours (Hardin, 2002: 4–5). The obligation of reciprocity that you have toward me, the obligation to return the favor, is, as the classical authors of social exchange theory considered, unspecified. That is, although I have an expectation of a future return of my favor, its exact nature is not specified in advance

(Blau, 1964: 93–94). In social exchange theory, the resources exchanged by the actors in a social network are considerably wide: they include all kinds of things that one actor possesses and that can be valued by other actors (Molm, 1997: 15).

The second condition supposes that the decision to trust generates an obligation to honor that trust in the trustee. Once again, it may have the effect of requiring the preservation of a certain reputation: the car dealer who wants to stay in business will try not to cheat his clients if certain conditions are met, especially the existence of sufficient information about the seller's behavior (Dasgupta, 1988: 61–63; Buskens and Weesie, 2000; Lahno, 1995; Kydd, 2000: 398; Heimer, 2001: 60). If the dealer does not honor the trust placed in him, he will lose not only the good opinion of the truster, but will also risk losing his reputation with anyone that learns about that behavior (Pettit, 1995: 216; Burt and Knez, 1995: 258). If a relation of trust exists between members of the same association, it might be expected that opportunistic behavior would readily be communicated by the person who has been cheated to other members of the group, or even to members of other social networks. This probably would destroy the opportunist's reputation. This is an example of the way in which closed networks or strong ties can make it easier to obtain information about the past behavior of other members of the network (Lin, 2001: 66). However, under these circumstances, only when reputation plays a role will trust generate an obligation to honor it. If there is no reputation to maintain, for example, when the relation of trust is not going to endure whatever the outcome, it can only be argued that the behavior of the trustee could be positively influenced by the idea that we rely on him. According to Karen Jones (1996), the expectation that trust is going to affect the trustee's behavior is a component of the idea of trust. To support this, she presents two arguments: first, often trust is not welcomed by the trustee, but what she rejects in this case is not the optimism of the truster in our goodwill but the expectation that we will feel influenced by the trust placed in us. Second, goodwill is often not influenced by the fact that someone relies on us (e.g., a doctor may look after us without being influenced by the fact that we depend on him). In my opinion, although trust is occasionally associated with the expectation that the trustee will be influenced by our decision to entrust her something, this is not an essential component of that decision. For example, in her first argument Jones assumes that trust is often rejected not because we do not honor the truster's beliefs about our goodwill, but because we do not honor the expectation that, after having trust placed in us, we will be influenced by that in our behavior. If that were the case, the decision to trust would imply two different expectations:

A. I expect that the trustee has goodwill; or
B. I expect that the trustee will be influenced by the fact that I trust
    him.

In my opinion, although it is true that both expectations are independent of each other, they are also to a certain extent incompatible. If we maintain expectation A, the decision to trust will be encouraged by the fact that I believe in the other person's trustworthiness. It is not necessary for this person to be influenced by my decision to trust them. In fact, in this case expectation B is not only unnecessary, but it might signal that I am not sure about the other's person goodwill. I expect that considerations (e.g., reputation) other than goodwill prevent them from cheating me.

Nevertheless, to bolster the idea that the behavior of the trustee could be positively influenced by the idea that we rely on him, consider the following mechanism. Let us suppose that breaking trust placed in you affects the idea that you have of yourself. Given that self-esteem is one of the most valuable goods, the reasoning would be as follows: if I trust you I send you a signal that, in my opinion, you have certain positive attributes, such as honesty. If you do not honor my trust, even if your reputation is saved (e.g., because, for whatever reason, I am not going to know that you have cheated me), your self-esteem may suffer. In this case, my trust on you could influence your behavior, given that this is something you might want to avoid. A historical example may help to clarify this argument. In 1858, Cavour and Napoleon III met in Plombières to discuss Italy's future. Cavour tried to convince Napoleon III to intervene against Austria. According to A. J. P. Taylor (1971), one of the arguments that Cavour used, which had most bearing on Napoleon's decision, was his trust in the emperor's revolutionary goodwill. Perhaps in this case it could be argued that Napoleon decided to go to war against Austria, among other reasons, to maintain France's reputation as a revolutionary power. Nevertheless, had he let down the kingdom of Sardinia, France's reputation would have remained intact, because, as Cavour himself pointed out, if France had a reputation, it was that of a Conservative power (at least since 1849 and the participation of France in the overthrowing of Mazzini's Roman Republic). Nor did the emperor have a strong reputation as a revolutionary to maintain in the wake of his personal collaboration in the overthrow of the Roman Republic. Nevertheless, all the evidence indicates that he saw himself as a revolutionary. In this example, betraying the Italian nationalists would not have had serious implications for France's position as a power, or for Napoleon's European reputation, but it was a decision that could not have been taken without damaging the emperor's image of himself. Trusting in Napoleon's revolutionary goodwill, Cavour generated in the emperor a certain obligation to be trustworthy. The mechanism illustrated by this example could operate when, for example, the temptation to break trust is not sufficiently strong, or when there are no mechanisms of self-deception at work (which allow us to think that we have a coherent set of values to defend, when actually we do not).

To sum up the arguments so far, I have contended that one way trust can generate resources of social capital is that it is associated with an obligation of reciprocity on the part of the trustee. This can be due to the need, under certain circumstances, to maintain a certain reputation, or to the influence that trust has on the behavior of the trustee. That is, trust generates social capital to the extent that the placement of trust supposes certain control on the trustee's future behavior. This is rather different from the two cornerstones of trust outlined by Hayashi et al. (1999). One of these is a benevolent conception of the cooperative nature of individuals. The other is a sense of control of the trustee's actions. This sense of control can help us to form expectations of trust, for example, that we will have more trust in those that we think we can control. But this might be entirely fictitious: in fact, it is possible that we exert no control at all. Only if we effectively exert that control can trust generate resources of social capital in the future. For example, Jean Mansbridge's (1999) "altruistic trust" could be seen as being founded on a particular sense of control of the trustee, when Mansbridge says that one of the possible altruistic reasons to trust is that my trusting behavior will be a model for other people, making them more trusting in similar situations. In this case, trust simply reflects a rather naive, pious feeling about other people's behavior, and it does not imply real control of the trustee's future behavior. This does not mean, however, that someone might think (erroneously) that in this way trusting you influences the behavior of others.

Another, complementary argument can be made for trust being a form of social capital. This thesis can best be understood if we focus on social or generalized trust. Social trust, which is analyzed in more detail in chapters 5 and 6, can be defined as trust in unknown people, that is, in people about whom we do not have any information about their trustworthiness. Someone who displays social trust will do favors for unknown people without expecting anything immediately in return, hoping that they or another unknown person will reciprocate in the future (Putnam, 2000: 134). This kind of trust can generate social capital in line with the first argument developed earlier: it will generate social capital if we suppose that the fact that we trust somebody generates in them an obligation to reciprocate, for whatever reason. As we see in chapter 3, this is a problematic assumption: in the case of social trust the incentives for violating that trust are especially high. Nevertheless, in chapter 5 I present some arguments to defend this assumption.

Now, it is worth considering this situation from the trustee's point of view. For the trustee, being part of a community characterized by high levels of social trust can be a source of social capital. When she trusts somebody, that trust will be honored. More obviously, when she needs a favor from her neighbor, she will obtain it. She can use the stocks of generalized trust inside the community to obtain resources of social capital, obligations of reciprocity or information. One surprising consequence of this way of looking at the role of social trust inside communities is that people outside the community can exploit these resources for negative ends. It is easy to see a community characterized by high levels of social trust as a community of "suckers" who are easy to exploit. In fact, citizens characterized by very high levels of social trust will be totally blind, for example, to corrupt behavior by their political leaders, something that draws into question the value of high levels of social trust for the effective functioning of a democracy.

To sum up, there are two ways of arguing that trust is a form of social capital. First, in terms of its source: relations of trust are generated through participation in social networks. Second, through reference to the fact that obligations of reciprocity are associated with a relation of trust. Both conditions are necessary for social capital, and neither of them is obvious. Here I have focused on the second of these arguments. The next chapters constitute, in a way, a defense of the first.

Information

Coleman argues that the informative potential of social networks is one form of social capital (1990: 310). Social relations that are maintained for other purposes, have as a by-product the collection of information. In this chapter, I consider two types of information that can be provided by participation in social networks: information about substantive issues (probably the type referred to by Coleman) and information about the preferences of members of the social network.

Participation in associations can, for example, provide information about issues unrelated to the specific aims of the association. Membership of an association for the protection of penguins, for example, might provide me with useful information about the genetic differences between species of penguins. Nevertheless, my fellow member, who also belongs to a public institution for environmental protection, may also provide me with equally useful information about job offers in that institution. This information is social capital, a resource that I obtain as a by-product of participation in an association. Another type of information, especially relevant to social capital literature, concerns the performance of politicians, something of great importance for all those who argue that social capital has beneficial effects on democracy (Putnam, 1993a; Pharr et al., 2000; Boix and Posner, 1996).

My social network influences the quantity and quality of information to which I have access. A large network of weak ties (between known people, but without relations of friendship) can provide me with more information about, for example, job offers, than a smaller network of friends (Granovetter, 1974). At the same time, a network of relations who have little contact with the real world can provide biased information. In 1913, for example, during the celebration of three centuries of Romanov rule in Russia, the tsarina confidently believed that the people loved the royal family and that the monarchy only had to remain close to the Russian people for them to open their hearts to the tsar and the tsarina (Figes, 2000: 45). In fact at that time hostility against the monarchy was widespread even among peasants. The tsarina's source of information included a clique of aristocrats with a remarkable capacity for self-delusion, and a group of deranged monks. This suggests that a network of strong ties, of friends and relatives, may not only provide less information (because their network is normally smaller than one formed exclusively by known people), but the quality of that information may also be poorer. My friends might, for example, have some interest in keeping hidden information that they consider harmful to me. Over and above this rather trivial example, it may be the case that information provided by individuals whose interests are different to mine is more useful. One problem with information provided by people with the same interests as me is that it may be of little use to me. That is, people who share my interests may have points of view that are very similar to mine, and, therefore, I might obtain very little new information from them. On the other hand, someone who does not share my interests, and who is not a member of my network of strong ties might provide me with more interesting information (Lin, 2001: 67). As Locke argues (1998: 386), first if I listen to those who disagree with me I may have more informed opinions and make better judgments. Second, it is possible that specific information provided by individuals of this type is more credible than the information provided by friends who share my interests. In particular, if an individual who does not share our interests provides us with information that conforms to our interests, we will normally consider this biased information to be more credible (Calvert, 1985). This type of individual is more likely to be found outside our network of strong ties. Nevertheless, I might want to exclusively use the information provided by my network of strong ties. One good reason for doing so (which might apply in the example of the tsarina) is also provided by Locke (1998: 420): if a person is afraid that an impartial opinion will run against the interests or prejudices of the receiver, she will tend to rely on opinions favorable to these interests and prejudices. This will lead, inevitably, to error.

The second kind of information, which has received less attention in the social capital literature, is information referring to the "type" of members of the social network. Information about type can be revealed, for example, through deliberation inside associations. Deliberation as discussion can reveal the participants' private information relating, for example, to their preferences. This kind of information can be relevant, as I show in chapter 4, for the establishment of relations of particularized trust. One problem of the revelation of the preferences of participants in the discussion is the possibility, if there are conflicts of interest within the association, of the existence of strategic incentives to misrepresent the revelation of preferences (Fearon, 1998: 46–47).[4] In any event, in most cases repeated interactions with members of the association will provide sufficient information about the type to which each member belongs.

It is now possible to summarize the main elements of my definition of social capital. In figure 2.1 I outline the main features of the definition of social capital that I have put forward in this chapter. Social capital involves obligations of reciprocity and information. Trust is associated with social capital, first, in that it is generated through participation in social networks, and, second, in that it creates an obligation of reciprocity in the trustee. In trying to clarify this relation I have advanced two possible mechanisms: the maintenance of a particular reputation by the trustee and the maintenance of his self-esteem. Both types of social capital are resources accessible by all participants in a social network: they can obtain favors in return for favors (obligations of reciprocity) and they can obtain information. Although this social capital is, as I argue in chapter 3, basically a by-product of actions with other ends, it can often be the outcome of a conscious decision: I can and will invest in social relations in order to retain resources of social capital.

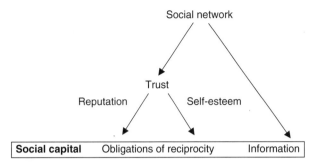

Figure 2.1   The social capital

This is the definition of social capital I use in this book. As I have said at the beginning of this chapter, my definition differs in some senses from some of the uses of the concept of "social capital" in political science. Those definitions usually assume that social capital is related to certain characteristics of individuals, more concretely, to their preferences and beliefs. Such preferences are usually related with civic virtue or "fraternity" (Funk, 1998; Booth and Richard, 1998; Shah, 1998: 470; Newton, 1997, 1999a). The authors that consider social capital a peculiar form of expectation or beliefs, identify it with the concept of "trust" and consider that trust as social capital is the effect of certain values or states of mood, like optimism (Whiteley, 1999; Green and Brock, 1998: 530–531), or the effect of a cultural norm (Sztompka, 1999: 66), or an affective attitude toward other people (Jones, 1996). My definition of social capital does not consider preferences or expectations as a form of capital, only obligations of reciprocity derived from relations of trust and information derived from participation in social networks. Those that analyze social capital as trust, although not sharing my definition of the concept, will nonetheless probably have some interest in the following chapters, given that I extensively analyze how to create social and particularized trust as sources of obligations of reciprocity and, thus, of social capital. However, the concept of trust that I use is ostensibly rooted in a rational choice framework and this is certainly not the norm in most of the analysis of trust in political science. The analysis of social capital as preferences, for example civic virtue, is faraway from my own definition of social capital. I think that some relation can be claimed between certain preferences traditionally considered as virtuous and trustworthiness. For example, for Cicero the virtuous man was gifted with the four cardinal virtues: prudence, justice, fortitude, and moderation. Justice is for

Cicero the "defense of human society" and the "observance of the fidelity to the contracts" (Cicero, *De Officiis* I: 15). This is clearly a characteristic related to trustworthiness. As Cicero himself said, justice is enough for trust: the good persons, fair and loyal, are never suspicious of fraud or injustice (Cicero, *De Officiis* II: 32–35). However, while it is true that certain preferences could be related to trustworthiness, it is doubtful that they could be related to trust: a virtuous person is no doubt trustworthy but this does not mean that she will also be trustful. Accordingly, preferences are excluded from my analysis of the different forms of trust (considered, as I have said, as an expectation) and, therefore, from the analysis of the different sources of social capital.

In this chapter I have presented the definition of social capital that I use in the rest of the book. This definition, as I have claimed, is somewhat different from many of the uses of the concept in the literature about social capital, especially that in political science. I now move on to the core of this work: the problem of the formation of social capital.

CHAPTER THREE

The Problem of the Formation of Social Capital

Introduction

As noted in chapter 2, social capital is a resource that promises to resolve some of the most important issues in social science (such as the relation between the "under-" and "super"-socialized views of human beings, as Coleman (1988) claimed), but also a wide variety of economic, political, and social problems. However, we know little about how this resource is created. Given that it is supposed to bring such great returns, the obvious question is: how can we invest in social capital?

In the remainder of this book, I seek to find an answer to this question. I begin this chapter by defining why investment in social capital is problematic. I consider the public-good features of some forms of social capital, in order to identify more precisely the problem of creating this kind of capital. In the rest of the book I suggest some ways in which these problems might be overcome.

The Public-Good Features of Social Capital in General

One of the peculiarities of social capital is that it has some of the features of a public good. A pure public good has two properties (Taylor, 1987: 5–6; Ostrom et al., 1994: 6–7):

(1) The difficulty of excluding individuals from benefiting from it; and
(2) The non-subtractability of the benefits consumed by one individual from those available to others.

According to James Coleman, social capital has features that differentiate it from private good and make it something more akin to a public good. On the one hand, it is a nonalienable good. Social capital, unlike physical or human capital, is not a property, but a resource accessible to all participants in a social network. This makes it difficult to trade. In fact, trust, whatever its effectiveness, for example, in easing economic exchange, is a kind of commodity on which it is impossible to put a price, or sell in an open market (Arrow, 1974: 23). Another difference with respect to private goods (including the other two forms of capital, human and physical), is that an individual who participates in the creation of social capital does not obtain all the returns from it, a factor that can lead to underinvestment in social capital (Coleman, 1990: 315–317). This second public-good feature of social capital, relating to the nonexclusivity of public goods, is especially interesting because it concerns one of the main attractions of the concept: social capital does not only benefit those who participate in its creation, but also has external effects on the wider community (Putnam, 2000: 20). It is precisely these externalities, typical of public goods, that make investment in these goods so complicated. Take, for example, the positive externalities that participation in associations has for democracy. Let us suppose, as Rosenstone and Hansen (1993) among others, argue, that it is true that participation in associations provides the participants with a by-product of relevant information that makes it easier to hold politicians accountable. Let us now imagine that a member of that association wins a prize in the lottery, and decides to move to his own private island, where the pleasures of associative life are not so widely appreciated. This decision supposes a payoff for him that clearly exceeds its costs. These costs include the loss in social capital that he suffers after abandoning his friends. Let us now imagine that all the members of the association, the lucky fellows, have also won prizes in the same lottery, and that all of them decide to move in search of better weather. From each of their individual points of view, their decision can be seen as correct, given that the cost for each of them in terms of the loss of social capital is clearly surpassed by the benefits of moving. Nevertheless, the aggregate outcome of these individual decisions could be a severe drop in the community's stock of social capital.

Coleman's conclusion is that, given that most of the benefits attached to actions relating to the creation of social capital are not enjoyed by those who create it, people are not interested in investing in social capital. This can encourage free-rider behavior. Let us suppose once more that the presence of all kinds of associations in a given community provides the members of those associations with the information they need to make the government more accountable. Let us further suppose that the outcome of this is a better democracy, with a government that is more accountable and more responsive to citizens' demands. There are benefits for each member of the community, whether the individual participates or not. There are, therefore, strong incentives to stay at home and not participate.

These problems associated with public good also affect a concept closely related to social capital: trust. First, consider the case of particularized trust, that is, trust between persons that know each other. A relationship of trust between two people can provide each of them with social capital. If one of them needs some money, for example, she can borrow it from her friend. Under certain circumstances, as we have seen in chapter 2, when she asks for the money, she assumes an obligation of reciprocity that is social capital in the hands of the lender. But it is possible that the original intention of the borrower was not to create these resources of social capital. In fact, if she could obtain that money in other ways, without asking for it from her friend, she would try to do so, and, as a result, social capital would not be created (Coleman, 1990: 316–317). This is a case in which, if there is a better option, the individual will not invest in social capital, given that part of the benefits of her investment goes to the creditor of the obligation of reciprocity. The decision to invest in social capital generates externalities for one of the parties to this relationship, something that, in certain circumstances, can lead to underinvestment. Generalized trust can also generate externalities. In Putnam's opinion (1993a), the communities of northern and central Italy show greater talent for the art of associative life than those in the south, precisely due to differences in generalized trust among citizens. According to this argument, if individuals trust in unknown people, it is more likely that they will decide to associate. This in turn is likely to have beneficial effects for the wider community and may, therefore, result in more efficient government. Additionally, according to Tocqueville (1996), participation in associations has positive economic consequences for the wider community because it generates individuals with more initiative. If one of the causes of participation in associations is social trust, its positive effects go beyond the truster, affecting even those individuals who do not believe that most people can be trusted.

Until this point, then, the free-rider problem in the creation of social capital. Given that part of the outcome of the investment in social capital benefits people who have not participated in that investment, as is the case with public goods, underinvestment is likely. This is true of social capital in the form of information, as well as of social capital derived from relations of trust. But this latter form of social capital is also exposed to another type of opportunist behavior, the consequence of a basic problem of asymmetric information. This problem of asymmetric information mainly concerns the "type" of trustee. It cannot be known in advance if the person is trustworthy, or an opportunist. And, in many cases, once the decision to cooperate has been made, say, based on high expectations of trust, the truster has to overcome the transaction costs attached to checking if the trustee has kept to the terms of the agreement or if she has cheated. These transaction costs lead us to another aspect of information asymmetry, relating not to the type of trustee, but to the actions she carried out in honoring the trust placed in her.

To a great extent, the importance of this opportunist behavior depends on the type of social network in which the trust relationship is embedded. If it is a social network that is likely to endure, as, for example, in the case of the traditional peasant communities analyzed by Michael Taylor (Taylor, 1988), the presence of opportunist behavior will be less frequent than in the case of a one-shot relationship. If the relationship is going to endure, individuals have an interest in being trustworthy. A similar solution provided by the transaction-costs literature is the preservation of reputation as a mechanism to fulfill agreements. The continuance of that specific relation is not necessary for this mechanism to operate, as it is sufficient that transactions of the same type are going to be frequent in the future, even if they are with different people. For example, if a certain agent has to make frequent transactions with different individuals and he is interested for whatever reason (say, because he is trying to sell something to each of those individuals) in maintaining their trust, he will be trustworthy (Kreps, 1990: 106–107; Burt and Knez, 1995: 258).[1] Another feature of the social network that can reduce opportunistic behavior is the degree to which it is closed. A closed network, in which each individual is related to all the others, can reduce opportunistic behavior by increasing the costs of opportunism. One good example is the case of the "Maghribi traders" analyzed by Avner Greif (1989). These tenth-century Mediterranean traders engaged in long-distance trade, carried out through agents. The problem was how to reduce the high transaction costs associated with monitoring agreements. In order to keep the agent honest, elements such as the agent's future discount factor, his reserve utility, or the probability of the trader monitoring the transaction all mattered. However, along with these factors, a key element in ensuring the agent remained trustworthy was the presence of a network of traders—with various degrees of relationship and friendship—who were committed to not hiring an agent that had cheated his principal. In this case, the closed nature of the social network strongly favored the agent's trustworthiness. Therefore, the shape of the social network affects the development and preservation of relations of trust, whether due to the continuance of the relations, or the degree to which the social network is closed. The implications, in terms of opportunistic behavior, of the type of social network are similar in the case of particularized trust and social trust. However, social trust also has some other distinctive features that foster opportunistic behavior. Social or generalized trust is trust in unknown people about whom no information about their trustworthiness is available. Anybody with those peculiar beliefs about other people's preferences will be easily cheated: they will tend to trust everybody. The trustees will have strong incentives to break this apparently ill-founded trusting behavior (Granovetter, 1985: 491). On the other hand, particularized trust is based on past experiences with other people, or on an evaluation of what behavior can be rationally expected from the other person given the incentives. That is, it is similar to Hardin's notion of trust as encapsulated interest (Hardin, 1993, 1996: 27, 2001, 2002). Opportunistic behavior is more easily avoidable in this case simply because the individual is less exposed to this kind of behavior.

In sum, there are basically two problems involved in the formation of social capital:

1. Underinvestment in social capital. Derived from the fact that the individual does not enjoy all the benefits attached to his investment in social capital. This is the most important similarity between social capital and public good.
2. Uncertainty about other people's preferences. Mainly relating to social or generalized trust. The trusting decision is made without full information about the trustee's type. Additionally, the monitoring of the fulfillment of agreements implies certain transaction costs.

How can the problems associated with the creation of social capital be overcome? In this chapter I discuss the answer generally put forward in the literature, namely that social capital is created as a by-product of other activities. I believe that this interpretation has a number of strengths, but is in itself insufficient. As shown in the chapters that follow, there are other ways of creating social capital.

The Most Common Response: The Creation of Social Capital as a By-Product

Due to its public-good features, it is difficult for social capital to be created in a direct way. That is why it is usually argued that social capital is created as a by-product of other activities (Coleman, 1988; Putnam, 1993a: 170).

Social capital is created as a by-product of activities relating to the obtainment of private good. In the case of private good, there is no collective-action problem as there are no incentives to free-ride. It is the same in the case of toll-goods (e.g., Putnam's famous bowling leagues), that is, a type of good characterized, like private good, by exclusivity, and, again like public good, by non-subtractability (Ostrom et al., 1994: 7). As a by-product of participation in private-good associations, individuals can obtain resources in the form of social capital. One of these resources could be the information-potential derived from relations inside those associations. Discussions within the association, for example, may serve to reveal private information to members of the association (Fearon, 1998: 46, 47). But it could also reveal other types of information. For example, if my fellow member is an expert in the stock exchange, I can make investments following his wise advice. Or I might be able to obtain information about job offers through the members of my "weak ties" network (Granovetter, 1974).

Although the creation of social capital as a by-product of participation in other activities seems to provide an adequate solution to our problem, it still has weaknesses.

A first question is: what accounts for the different stocks of social capital between communities? If social capital is the by-product of a wide range of activities, from participation in associations to membership of a more or less dense network of friends, we do not really know why some communities are blessed with higher levels of social capital than others.

One possible answer to this puzzle is that put forward by Putnam in *Making Democracy Work*. Putnam believes that the difference between the networks of civic engagement found in the north and south of Italy can be explained by the existence of different attitudes toward participation, which is a consequence of different cultural traditions. Putnam traces these cultural differences back to the eleventh century, when a series of city-states developed in the center and north of Italy that fostered the active participation of citizens in public affairs. In the same period, southern Italy fell into the hands of the Norman monarchy, thereby succumbing to a pattern of feudalism, lack of political autonomy in ancient cities like Naples and Amalfi, clientelism, and political apathy.

In my opinion, Putnam's cultural explanation for the origins of social capital suffers from a number of flaws. The most important of these is his use of sociohistorical studies in his analysis. This is based exclusively, as has been pointed out by various critics, on a poor research using secondary sources (Cohn, 1994; Sabetti, 1996; Brucker, 1999). His description of political life in the northern Italian city-states is highly idealized, while his description of the south is excessively negative. His treatment of the period from the decadence of the northern city-states to the establishment of fascism is superficial. He overlooks the effects of Spanish rule in the south (Naples and Sicily) and in the center and north (Milan, and Spain's client-states of Tuscany and Genoa), and fails to take account of the effects of the reforms introduced in the course of the Enlightenment and the *Risorgimento* on the associations typical of the *Ancién Régime*. One wonders why the civic traditions of southern trading cities (such as Amalfi, which had developed republican institutions, such as the election of the *dux* by lot, by the ninth century (Kreutz, 1996: 89)) succumbed to the Normans, while civic traditions in the north and center of Italy survived, for example, the Spanish viceroys. In fact, as has been pointed out by Padgen (1988), a common argument in the eighteenth-century Neapolitan's Enlightenment was about the negative effects of the Spanish rule in Italy. One of these supposed effects was the substitution of a society based on trust by one based on honor. The Spanish viceroys were conscious destroyers of social capital. Although the argument that the Spanish viceroys consciously replaced trust by honor is historically problematic, I think that it is enough to say that Spanish rule destroyed civic traditions and institutions in Italy, consolidating the aristocratic rule in the peninsula. But this effect was felt both in the south and in northern Italy. The duchy of Milan was a Spanish possession during nearly two centuries, there were Spanish garrisons (*presidios*) in Tuscany, and the minor Italian states of the center and north of the peninsula were Spain's clients. The loyalty to the Spanish king of the rulers of these minor states was assured by annual bribes from Madrid. In fact, as it is well known to every reader of Machiavelli's *Dell'arte de la Guerra* and the *Discorsi*, the destruction of the republic of Florence's civic institutions in 1512 was due to the action of the Spanish troops.

Moreover, it is not clear whether Putnam was in fact trying to explain different patterns of social capital formation. Going back to the eleventh century to explain the differences in social capital between Italian regions might have been useful if it had, first, identified the explanatory factors that accounted for the initial differences in social capital between north and south. It would have been more convincing, second, if he had plausibly argued that these initial differences created a "virtuous circle" in the north and a "vicious circle" in the south, circles that survived through the centuries and across political regimes, from Spanish rule to fascism. Putnam does not draw these conclusions, however, partly due to the difficulties involved in demonstrating the persistence of civic traditions across centuries. As Putnam himself acknowledges, the dynamics as well as initial differences in social capital between north and south remain unexplained (Putnam, 1993a: 180).

The historical chapter of *Making Democracy Work* does not, therefore, constitute an attempt to explain different patterns of social capital formation, but rather a failed defense of the existence of path dependence in history. As a consequence, the problem of the formation of social capital persists. The argument that social capital is created as a by-product is incomplete, since it fails to account for differences in social capital between communities.

In the following chapters, I build on the commonly held position that views social capital, essentially, as a by-product of other activities. In general terms, I consider that, although particularized trust is essentially a by-product of other activities, social trust may have other sources. Among these, I emphasize the role of the State. Finally, I put forward a possible explanation for the generation of "virtuous circles" of social capital creation. Although an understanding of specific historical cases is not the aim of this book, I argue that my interpretation may help to explain the differences in social capital between northern and southern Italy discussed by Putnam.

CHAPTER FOUR

The Creation of Particularized Trust

In this chapter I analyze how particularized trust is created inside networks, focusing my attention on voluntary associations. Particularized trust, that is, trust in known people, constitutes an example of how social capital can be created as a by-product of other activities. Here I propose a general mechanism to explain how particularized trust is created as a by-product. This mechanism involves the disclosure of private information within associations. However, I also identify difficulties with this method of creating particularized trust. One concerns the uncertainty of the information thus acquired, another is the possibility of misjudging this information due to certain cognitive processes, and a third the reliability of the information obtained. Therefore, this is a chapter about the creation of a particular form of trust but also, as it was derived from chapter 2, about the creation of social capital inside associations. As we know, this is so because the relations of trust created inside associations are sources of obligations of reciprocity, that is, of social capital. I assume in this chapter that the relations of trust created between members of a given association are a quasi automatic source of obligations of reciprocity (and, therefore, of social capital), through the operation of at least the two mechanisms presented in chapter 2: reputation and self-esteem.

As noted earlier, particularized trust is mainly created as a by-product of other activities. Associations, in particular, are considered to be the privileged locus of creation of particularized trust as a by-product. Let's take Putnam's favorite example: a bowling league. It is assumed that between games members of the association create relations of trust. As a result, if one of the members of the association needs a favor, she can rely on her colleagues, given that they know that the favor will be reciprocated. The mechanism for this trust relation is the information obtained about the other players' type. The type, in terms of a signaling game, relates to any kind of private information. In this case, it could be private information about the preferences of the other player. Trust is, after all, an expectation, a belief about the other players' strategies. Repetitive interactions should provide information about the other players' type. That is, we should learn if the other player is trustworthy, if she returns favors, or if, given the opportunity, she acts as a free-rider. Thanks to this information, each player can update her expectations about when to trust. It is a type of "particularized trust," a trust in known people (Uslaner, 1999: 124). Note that this does not mean that participation in an association inevitably generates systems of trust. In fact, the information obtained is in itself neutral. The updating of expectations could in fact run against relations of trust. For example, day-to-day interactions might tell me that my bowling colleague is not only incapable of winning a game, but also that she will not return my money if I lend her ten euros. Nonetheless, the revelation of the type raises the likelihood of relations of trust, because cooperators can recognize each other.

In this case, therefore, the source of trust is information about the past behavior of members of my social network. It is the "street-level" source of trust (Hardin, 1993). Although we do not have all the information available about the behavior of known individuals, and therefore cannot predict with confidence what their future behavior will be, past information is enough to form plausible expectations about such future behavior.[1] This can, of course lead to error. People change, and yesterday's good type can be tomorrow's bad type. Or it may be the case that, given sufficiently strong incentives, everybody would betray his or her best friend.

A rather different case of information acquired about the other individual type being irrelevant occurs when we adapt our expectations about the other party to our feasible set, disregarding new information. This is a variant of Elster's argument about "sour grapes" (1983). According to Elster, in some cases the feasible set determines the preferences. Given that the fox cannot reach the grapes, he concludes that he does not really want them because they are sour. The change of preference takes place through a psychological mechanism of cognitive dissonance reduction. Perhaps this same process also takes place in the case of beliefs.

To illustrate this point, we can consider the example of Hitler and Chamberlain, a historical case that fits this idea well. Between his rise to power in 1933 and the Munich Crisis in 1938, Hitler had denounced the Versailles Treaty, reintroduced obligatory conscription, began full-scale rearmament, remilitarized the Rhineland, intervened in the

Spanish Civil War, and, finally, annexed Austria. Before each of these acts, which almost inevitably led to war, Hitler had repeatedly denied that he had any plans for external aggression. The day before German troops entered Vienna, he announced that he only wanted a pacific monetary union with Austria. Nevertheless, in spite of all the obvious signals that indicated that Hitler was untrustworthy, the British prime minister, Neville Chamberlain, affirmed in a letter to his sister on September 19, 1938 that "in spite of his roughness and the implacability I saw in his face, I had the impression that he is someone to trust after giving his word" (Kershaw, 2000: 129). This statement can be interpreted as proof of Chamberlain's lack of intelligence, or of his naivete. Yet he was not naive in his dealings with the British labor movement, although he might not be considered a particularly outstanding politician. His trust in Hitler can in fact be explained in a different way. He might have thought that Britain was unprepared for war. In other words, that he could not afford the consequences that Hitler, after all, was untrustworthy. Given that this conclusion was too dreadful, he decided that the fascist dictator was trustworthy. Perhaps saying that he "decided" that Hitler was trustworthy is going too far. If that were the case, it would be an example of implausible self-deception. Self-deception implies that the individual intentionally ignores what he really believes, and assumes an easier or more comforting belief. That is, an example of "believing at will." The problem, as Elster (1983) argues, is that it is not very clear how we can intentionally hide plausible beliefs, and, at the same time, believe in non-plausible beliefs. Elster's alternative to self-deception, an alternative that may be applicable to the example of Hitler and Chamberlain, is the rationalization of hope. Rationalization of hope is an unconscious impulse and, although it cannot be causally rooted on the available information, it can at least be supported by that information. Although Chamberlain did not have information showing that Hitler was trustworthy, he could point to some relatively weak evidence (mainly, Hitler's public declarations) to update consciously his beliefs about the type of fascist dictator he was dealing with.

To further clarify Chamberlain's decision to cooperate with Hitler, it might be useful to compare it with that of his colleague, the French prime minister, Edouard Daladier. When Daladier went to Munich in 1938 to approve the cession to Germany of parts of Czechoslovakia, it does not seem that he was very optimistic about Hitler's trustworthiness. Like Chamberlain, Daladier was frankly pessimistic about the possibilities of defeating Germany in the event of war. Because of that, his decision to cooperate with Hitler was determined by the benefits of that decision in terms, say, of the time it gave France to prepare for war. But he did not update his expectations about Hitler's type. This is an example of how the relationship between the feasible set, the potential gains, and the potential losses affect the decision to cooperate. The case of Chamberlain is different, however. Chamberlain's decision to cooperate was not only based on the potentially high payoffs if Hitler was trustworthy but, more importantly, on his high expectations about Hitler's trustworthiness induced by the fact that the potential losses in the case that he were not trustworthy were so great.

In this example, the information about the other's type is not taken into account by considerations relating to the feasible set. In other cases, the information obtained is not taken into account because it does not seem credible due to the position of each party to the relation in the social network. This is the case, superficially considered in the social capital literature (e.g., in Putnam (1993a: 173–175), and Stolle (1998: 501)) of vertical associations. According to Putnam (1993a: 175), in a vertical relation opportunistic behavior is more likely by both the patron (exploitation) and the client (shirking). On the other hand, he suggests that horizontal relations foster strong norms of reciprocity, ease of communication and the flow of information about the trustworthiness of others (Putnam 1993a: 173–174).

These arguments are, in any event, insufficient. In this chapter I consider the extent to which hierarchical relations constitute an obstacle to the development of trust. First, I present my arguments about the obstacles for the development of relations of trust inside hierarchical undemocratic organizations. These arguments are further developed in a game theoretic model. Second, I present a historical example that illustrates the main points of the game. Finally, I test the validity of the hypotheses using survey data.

There are two features of hierarchical organizations that make the development of trust less likely in horizontal ones: the asymmetries in information and distribution of power among the members of the organization.

A typical vertical organization is characterized by the presence of information asymmetries among its members. Imagine, for example, the capitalist enterprise. In this kind of enterprise, the owner lacks information about the performance of the worker. In this sense, the capitalist enterprise has been highlighted as a classic example of a game with asymmetric information (Rasmusen, 1989: 133–221). In a typical production game, the worker has to perform some task for the owner of the firm. Although the owner can observe the outcome, he cannot observe the worker's efforts and this cannot be directly inferred from the outcome, given that this outcome could be the result of various variables, and not just individual effort (Miller, 1992: 121). The owner, therefore, has insufficient information about the workers' efforts. This situation can be approached from another angle. Suppose that, alleging financial problems, the owner decides to dismiss a number of his employees as the only way of avoiding bankruptcy. It could be that the remaining workers lack sufficient information to determine whether the owner has deceived them or told them the truth. In this case, asymmetric information can be a barrier to the development of trust. If none of the players has full information about the other players' preferences, mutual distrust seems more likely than mutual trust. How can this obstacle be overcome? Gary Miller's (2001) answer is credible commitments. Miller assumes that trust is necessary inside firms, because it fosters efficiency. Workers are more ready to make personal investments, such as investment in firm-specific human capital, if they trust that their managers are not going to dismiss them for profit-maximization in the short term. To obtain the workers' trust, Miller's solution is the delegation of key decisions by the owner to a manager with different preferences: for example, the maximization of productivity, rather than profit-maximization in the short term (Miller, 2001: 320). In my opinion, the problem with this commitment is that it lacks credibility: the owner can dismiss the manager if and when he again comes to adopt short-term profit-maximization as a priority. Another possible solution is for the owner to send signals to his subordinates about his trustworthiness. For example, the so-called efficiency wage (a wage higher than that of the Walrasian equilibrium paid for efficiency reasons) is taken by Wielers (1997) as a signal of trust by the employer in his employees. However, for various reasons, such as envy due to wage differentials between superiors and subordinates, the credibility of this signal for the employee is always dubious (Miller, 1992: 196).

What is the main problem with the credibility of these kinds of commitments in vertical organizations? In my opinion, and as mentioned earlier, it is the presence of power asymmetries between the parties to the relation. Consider once again the example of the capitalist enterprise. According to Marxists, the capitalist firm is not only characterized by asymmetric information, but also by asymmetric power.[2] According to Bowles and Gintis (1990: 182), "the entrepreneur A has power over the worker B, given that A can use a threat of sanction to compel B to act in A's interest, whereas the contrary is not true." This asymmetric power helps to make the hierarchical superior's commitments less credible. If he has committed himself not to dismiss employees if there are financial difficulties, or not to reduce the piece-rates in response to an increase in productivity (Miller, 2001: 314–315), he nevertheless has the power to renege on his word. The hierarchically inferior parties do not have the power to sanction the employers, so his commitment is not credible. Now let us take the relation the other way round. As noted earlier, in capitalist firms employers do not have full information about their employees' efforts. They have reasons to distrust their employees in this respect. But they also have the power to sanction their employees (from small pecuniary sanctions to dismissal) if they can prove that the employees have not done their work. Although this does not fully eliminate his information problem, his power to sanction his hierarchical inferiors is a guarantee of trust.

One reasonable objection to these arguments about hierarchical organizations is that voluntary organizations, even hierarchical ones, are not exactly like firms. This is true, but my contention is that they are more or less similar in the relevant sense for my arguments. That is, if it can be claimed that hierarchical voluntary organizations are also plagued with asymmetries in power and information, then this would be enough to meet my arguments. Consider, for example, a political party. This is a kind of voluntary organization that is seen in most of the cases as internally undemocratic. The asymmetric information between the leadership and the rank and file members lies in the fact that the leadership retain private information about, say, the party's hidden agenda if it reaches power. The asymmetries in power between the leaders and the rank and file members are embodied in the lack of effective mechanisms of accountability. Given the presence of these asymmetries, the argument runs, distrust is likely to arise between the leadership and the rank and file.

Thus, we can argue that vertical organizations are less prone to the development of particularized trust. Although there are at least as many conflicting preferences in vertical organizations as in horizontal ones, there are two important differences in vertical organizations that impede the achievement of a trusting equilibrium: the presence of asymmetries in information and of power between the two sides of the organization (Herreros and Criado, 2003).

In order to illustrate the problem of trust in an undemocratic hierarchical organization, I first consider the case of the Mafia, one of Putnam's favorite examples of a vertical organization, and one that since Gambetta has been extensively studied in the literature on trust. I propose a trust game between a Mafia boss and his henchman. It is an agency game with incomplete, imperfect, and asymmetric information. This game is depicted in figure 4.1. Second, I provide a historical example to further

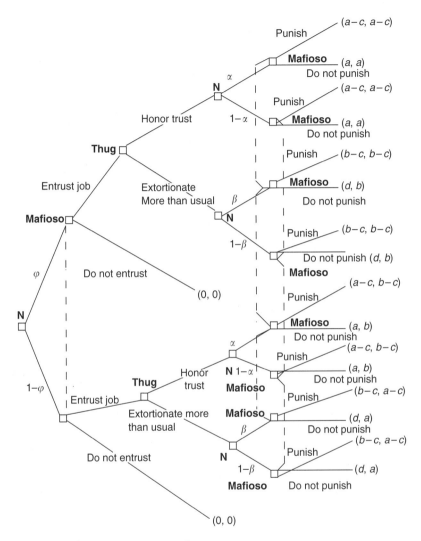

Figure 4.1   The trust game as an agency's game

illustrate the case for the existence of special obstacles in a hierarchical and undemocratic organization for the development of trust. This historical example is the Soviet Terror process in 1937–38.

We begin with the game of figure 4.1. The Mafioso orders an agent (his henchman) to do certain jobs he himself is unwilling to do.

For example, to extort money from a local shopkeeper. His information problem is that he cannot directly observe if his hood keeps part of the extortion money for himself by demanding more than the usual amount from the shopkeeper. However, the Mafia has been shown in recent studies to be an organization that effectively resolves its trust problem (Gambetta, 1988b). The solution, once again, lies in the threat of sanctions. Given that the sanctions employed by the Mafia also tend to be rather unpleasant, hoods will prefer to be honest with their bosses. Nevertheless, this does not eliminate the information problem altogether. Regardless of whether the decision-making process in the hierarchy is centralized or not, information problems remain. But even in this case, the hierarchical superior can use a combination of monitoring and sanction to make his subordinates trustworthy. This, however, is something beyond the reach of his subordinates. These arguments are shown in the game in figure 4.1. In accordance with Putnam's idea of the Mafia as a model of hierarchical relation, I consider two players in this game: the Mafioso and his henchman. The latter can be one of two types: loyal or disloyal. The difference between the two types is that, although both of them are prepared under certain circumstances to betray their boss, the former believes the myth that the Mafia is an honorable institution, and, accordingly, betrayal would represent a cost for him, whereas the latter knows that "it is just business." The Mafioso considers that his thug is loyal with probability φ, and disloyal with probability $1 - \varphi$. He sends his henchman to extort money from a local shopkeeper. The henchman can honor the trust placed on him, or extort more money than usual, keeping the difference. Unfortunately for the boss, he cannot directly observe if his henchman has fulfilled his duty as a good hood. Nevertheless, he can observe an outcome that can help him decide if his hood is loyal or not. The extorted shopkeeper may be tempted to go to the police. The probability of the shopkeeper going to the police is denoted by a nature's move, in which the higher branch indicates that he has actually gone to the police, and the lower branch, that he has not gone. The boss is not very worried about this probability, because he lives in a community characterized by the practical absence of social capital, one of the unpleasant effects of which is a corrupt police force. In any event, if the shopkeeper goes to the police, this might indicate that he has been extorted more than usual, or simply that he has been brave enough to report the incident. The Mafioso knows that the probability of the police coming to the "scene of the crime" is α if the thug has done his work well, and β if he has extortionated more than usual, and he also knows that $\beta > \alpha$. He has to figure out whether the thug has cheated him or not using the police as a signal. After the nature move that indicates the probability of the police coming to investigate, he can either punish or not punish his thug. The Mafioso obtains a payoff a if the thug does his job well and he does not punish him. If he punishes him, his payoffs are reduced by $-c$. If the Mafioso punishes an untrustworthy thug, his payoffs are $b - c$. Finally, if he fails to punish the untrustworthy thug, he obtains a payoff denoted by d. The trustworthy thug obtains his maximum payoffs, denoted by a, if he honors trust and the Mafioso does not punish him. If he is punished, he obtains a payoff denoted by $a - c$. He will prefer this to cheating the Mafioso (he erroneously believes, after seeing Coppola's *The Godfather* that the Mafia is an organization based on honor). In this case, he will obtain a payoff denoted by b. His last preference is to cheat the Mafioso and be punished, in which case his payoffs are $b - c$. What about the untrustworthy thug? He is not as idealistic as the other type of thug. He knows that "it is just business." His first preference is to cheat the Mafioso and escape without a sanction (a). He prefers this to being sanctioned ($a - c$). His last two preferences are honor trust (for him, this means being a sucker) (b), and honor trust and be punished ($b - c$).

When will the two types of thugs honor the trust placed on them? All depends on the Mafioso's strategy. The Mafioso has five strategies. He can, first, not entrust the thug a job. Second, he can entrust him a job and punish him whether the police come or not. Third, he can entrust him a job and punish him only if the police come. Fourth, he can entrust him the job and punish him only if the police does not come. And finally, he can entrust him a job and punish him whatever the police does. We can discard two of the strategies: do not punish ever and punish only when the police does not come, as clearly inferior to the others. One strategy is intuitively attractive to the Mafioso: entrust the thug a job and punish him just when the police come. The Mafioso can consider the police as a signal that the thug has betrayed him, taking into account that $\beta > \alpha$. Being p (Thug betrays/Police come) the conditional probability that the thug has betrayed the Mafioso given that the police has come, the Mafioso's strategy of entrusting the thug a job and then punishing him if the police come is preferred to the other strategies when p (Thug betrays/Police come) $> (a + b - d - c)/(b - c - d) > 0$. The Mafioso updates his priors $(1 - \varphi)$ of the thug being untrustworthy after the police come. If the probability the Mafioso assigns to the thug being untrustworthy if the police come is sufficiently high, he will punish the thug. If this is the case, what will the thug do? Whether he is trustworthy or untrustworthy, he will honor trust when the probability of the police coming if he betrays the Mafioso is sufficiently high. This probability has to be $\beta > (a - b)/c + \alpha$ for the untrustworthy thug, and $\beta > (b - a)/c + \alpha$ for the loyal type.

This game illustrates the fact that hierarchical relations represent an obstacle to the development of trust between subordinates and their superiors. Nonetheless, the game also illustrates that the presence of sanctions facilitates the fulfillment by the subordinates of the trust placed on them. The thug will comply with his orders because he knows that if he does not there is a possibility of being sanctioned by the Mafioso.

In short, hierarchical relations represent an obstacle to the development of trust of subordinates in their superiors, although the presence of sanctions makes a similar decision by superiors less risky. A further argument is that a hierarchical superior will be interested in blocking the development of trust relations between his subordinates. For example, an employer could be interested in hiring an ethnically heterogeneous workforce in order to hamper labor organization (Bowles and Gintis, 1990: 185–186). On the other hand, in horizontal relations, at least one of the obstacles to the development of trust in vertical relations is absent: asymmetric power relations. In an ideal horizontal organization, the leaders are accountable to the members. The absence of accountability in vertical organizations is a key factor in explaining the absence of relations of trust between superiors and subordinates. This alone explains why in horizontal relations the obstacles to the development of trust are lower, because, even if it is entirely clear that information asymmetries and interest conflict are lower in horizontal relations, it is clear that they are, at least, not higher. Next, I present an example of the game of figure 4.1 in motion, although in this case not referred to the Italian Mafia. The example is generally considered as an extreme case of pathological distrust inside an organization: the Terror process in the Soviet Union, especially inside the Soviet Communist Party, during the years 1937–38. In the course of 15 months during these years 1937–38, 1,565,000 people, according to official figures, were arrested in the Soviet Union, of whom about 700,000 were executed (Jansen and Petrov, 2002: 104). Some of them were high rank members of the Soviet Communist Party—including nearly all of the old Bolsheviks that carried out the October Revolution alongside Lenin—but most of them were rank and file members of the Party and ordinary Soviet citizens, selected on an arbitrary basis. All these people were forced (using all kind of pressures) to confess imaginary crimes against the State and the Soviet leadership. In some cases they were obliged to make their confessions in public. Although all the authors agree that the origins of the Terror were in Stalin's desire to retain power as the dictator of the Soviet State, the strange peculiarities of the Terror have been explained using different arguments. Most commonly, they are attributed to Stalin's irrationality. For example, Robert Tucker considered that certain features of Stalin's mind, especially his self-hate and self-condemnation for failing short of his ideal self's standards of perfection, led him to find relief by turning this self-hate outward against others (Tucker, 1990: 162). Alan Bullock agrees with Tucker in that Stalin's brutal treatment by his father "produced a basic anxiety, the sense of being isolated in a hostile world, which can lead a child to develop a neurotic personality" (Bullock, 1998: 12). According to Amy Knight, this abusive treatment by his father "left Stalin with an inherent distrust of other people and a strong vindictive streak, traits that were reinforced by Georgian societal norms" (Knight, 1993: 6). Other aspects of Stalin's personality are brought forward to explain some of the apparently extravagant features of the mass Terror. For example, the arbitrariness of the repression is sometimes interpreted as the product of his pathological distrust, which led him to practice brutal violence not just toward everything that opposed him but also toward that which seemed to his capricious and despotic character contrary to their concepts (Conquest, 1990: 66; Chamberlain, 1956: 240–241). In general, Stalin's regime has been portrayed as "a piece of prodigious insanity" (Deutscher, 1984: 326) or as "the art of governance typical of a mental hospital" (Service, 1997). As we can see, Stalin's irrational, pathological distrust has been considered as an important explanatory variable of the Terror process. This image of Stalin has been transmitted also by some of his collaborators during this period. For example, according to Khrushchev (cited in Conquest, 1990: 56): "(…) Stalin was a very distrustful man, sickly suspicious: we knew this from our work with him. He could look at a man and say: 'Why are your eyes so shifty today?' or 'Why are you turning so much today and avoiding looking me directly in the eyes?'. The sickly suspicion created in him a general distrust even towards eminent party workers whom he had known for years. Everywhere and in everything he saw 'enemies,' 'double-dealers' and 'spies.'"

One way to explain the Terror is, then, to assume that Stalin had irrational expectations about other people's trustworthiness. In fact, this hypothesis has been backed with even some medical evidence (one, by the way, that reminds me of a glorious similar joke in Woody Allen's film *Everyone Says I Love You*). According to one of the doctors who examined Stalin's body after his death in March 1953: "I suggest that Stalin's cruelty and suspiciousness, his fear of enemies, loss of adequacy in assessing people and events and his extreme obstinacy were all created to some extent by the arteriosclerosis of the cerebral arteries (…) An essentially sick man was managing the State" (Knight, 1993: 172).

However, this kind of explanation implies some problems. One is that it cannot explain adequately some extravagant features of the Terror process: for example, its arbitrariness. Everybody could be a victim of the Terror. On July 30, 1937, People's Commissar Nikolai Ezhov, chief of the NKVD, the State Security forces, presented to the Politburo the order number 0047, "Concerning the Operation Aimed at the Subjecting to Repression of Former Kulaks, Criminals and Other Anti-Soviet Elements." This order divided the target of the repression in two categories. The first category comprised the most hostile elements, who were to be immediately arrested and shot. The second category comprised those who, after the arrest, were to be confined in camps and prisons for a term ranging from eight to ten years. The troikas constituted in each republic and province to implement the order had to fulfill a certain quota of arrests for each category and had the right to request an enlargement of the quotas. In fact, they were even encouraged to do so (Jansen and Petrov, 2002: 87–90).

At first sight, the victims of the repression had some characteristics in common, like social origins, past or present posts, relationship or friendship with someone, nationality or connection with a foreign country, or activity in specific Soviet organizations (Conquest, 1990: 270–271). However, this did not exclude arbitrariness in the repression—it was assumed it would be so up to a certain point. On the contrary, the arbitrariness of the arrests would be one of the most striking features of the mass Terror. The process was the following: as the troikas had to fulfill a given quota, they needed a good starting point for the arrests. This could be, for instance, social origins. After the first wave of arrests, the acquaintances of the arrested could be arrested too, then their acquaintances and so on. In fact, all kinds of people could end up in the camps, or being shot. In Ezhov's words, "a certain number of innocent people will be annihilated too (…) if during this operation an extra thousand people will be shot, that is not such a big deal" (Jansen and Petrov, 2002: 84). That is, some arrested people were truly innocent and the officials that arrested them knew, as a matter of fact, that they were so.

My point here is that, in fact, distrust inside the Communist Party organization was not that irrational. This distrust derived from the hierarchical character of the Party's organization. As I have claimed in this chapter, a hierarchical organization generates distrust in two ways: by information asymmetries and by power asymmetries. However, the leadership of the Soviet Communist Party—that is, Stalin and his closest collaborators, like Molotov or Ezhov, could rely in the Soviet State's capacity to sanction those in the lower levels of the Communist Party's organization in order to manage their distrust. The reasons for Stalin's distrust laid in two facts: the likely preferences of some of the members of the Communist Party and the information asymmetries about those preferences. It is reasonable to think that many members of the Communist Party were dissatisfied with Stalin's policies in the 1930s, especially the collectivization and the radical industrialization processes. In general terms, the indifference and tacit acceptance of the Soviet government during the 1920s was turned into hostility during the 1930s. During the 1930–32 period, the collectivization process and the subsequent famine brought enormous suffering to the Soviet peasants, who therefore resisted collectivization (Conquest, 1986: 154–155). After the failure of the 1936 harvest, there was a "winter of discontent" for the peasantry in various parts of Russia (Davies, 1997: 55). Regarding the workers, despite a modest improvement in their living standards during the second five-year plan, for most of them the immediate priority in the 1930s was sheer survival (Davies, 1997: 23). Although it seems that discontent was less widespread among workers than among peasants, there were obvious sources of discontent in the bad economic situation and the lack of *glasnost* for both (Davies, 1997: 41). This discontent could have been exploited by political entrepreneurs inside the Party (e.g., the old Bolsheviks) to overthrow Stalin's tyranny. There was some ground, then, to believe that some members of the Party could be conspiring to overthrow Stalin's leadership. However, there were information asymmetries inside the Party to discover this anti-Stalinist cadres and rank and file members of the Party. The likely presence of these people inside the Party was combined with a low capacity of the State apparatus to discover real opposition to Stalin's policies. This incapacity was especially felt in the countryside. In the 1920s and the 1930s the Party was extraordinarily weak in the villages. In 1928, as Molotov complained, agricultural workers and poor peasants only made up 5 percent of the Party's membership (Conquest, 1986: 103). Transports and communications were defective and the representatives of the State outside the cities were very few (Getty and Naumov, 1999). Actually, the replacement of Yagoda by Ezhov as chief of the NKVD could have been partly motivated by the low efficiency of the Soviet security forces (Getty and Naumov, 1999). The information asymmetries inside the Party reminds us of those same asymmetries in a capitalist enterprise: the rank and file members of the Party could not make the leadership accountable for its policies but the leadership also lacked information about the rank and file members' activities. The likely outcome of these asymmetries was distrust by both the leadership and the rank and file members. Nevertheless, the leader had a card to play to better manage distrust: to use his power to sanction his subordinates. In my view, that is precisely the role of the Terror. In the game of figure 4.1, we have seen that the Mafioso keeps his thug loyal to him because there is one possibility of being sanctioned if the thug cheats the Mafioso. In that game, the Mafioso had not all the information he needed about his thug's activities but he could rely in a signal—the coming of the police—to update his expectations about the thug's trustworthiness. Stalin was not so lucky. He lacked information, like the Mafioso, about the Party member's type but he could not rely in any signal to discover it. For this reason, he relied instead on arbitrary Terror. However, he could not simply rely on arbitrary Terror. If the Terror was arbitrary, the probability of being detained would have been the same with or without conspiring against Stalin and the opposition to Stalin would have conspired against the leadership anyway. To avoid this situation, Stalin used the public trials. Although Terror was arbitrary, Stalin had an interest in making people believe that it was not so but that the Soviet courts were condemning real conspirators, spies, and wreckers. This was necessary for people to think that the probability of being detained if conspiring against the Soviet regime was higher than if not. To achieve this, Stalin insisted in obtaining confessions by all means from the innocent people arrested by the NKVD.

Thus, given the hierarchical and undemocratic character of the Soviet Communist Party, distrust between leadership and rank and file members was the most likely outcome. Some members of the Party were against Stalin's policies but information asymmetries inside the organization prevented Stalin from knowing exactly who they were. Distrust was a rational expectation for Stalin to have, given this situation. The Terror was a device to manage this distrust and, given the general lack of information, arbitrary Terror and public confessions of imaginary crimes was a good strategy to remain in power. Although Stalin's preferences (to retain power at all costs, even the lives of hundreds of thousands) were monstrous and, in a sense, hardly rational, his expectations about their comembers of the Party's trustworthiness were not irrational but derived from the features of the Party's organization. Consequently, the strategy to manage distrust was a rational, although implacable, means to achieve his preferences.

According to the theoretical arguments and examples I have presented so far, we would expect, then, particularized trust (i.e., trust between members of a given organization) to flourish more easily in horizontal than in vertical organizations. This hypothesis has scarcely been empirically tested because of the lack of adequate survey data. This is my next task: to test empirically whether horizontal organizations provide more favorable settings for the development of particularized trust than vertical ones. In order to carry out this task, I use a survey that includes one variable relating to trust in members of an association and a second relating to the degree of participation of members in the decision-making process. It is the *Barómetro de opinión publica de Andalucía* (Barometer of Andalusian Public Opinion) of 2000 (IESAA/CSIC). This is a survey with a sample size of 3,645. It is a large enough survey to include a number of individuals who belong to horizontal and vertical associations. One possible objection to the use of this data is that some of the possible effects that we could find are the consequence of specific regional characteristics. However, Andalusia is the largest region of Spain and its degree of economic development is very similar to the southern European's mean. Their representative institutions are perfectly assimilable to European ones. Nevertheless, the use of a multivariable estimation allows me to isolate the effects of the characteristics of the type of association in the development of particularized trust from the impact of sociodemographic characteristics, such as income or education. In this survey I have included a question relating to the decision-making process inside associations. From the responses to this question, I have built a proxy of a type of organizational arrangement (vertical vs. horizontal). I have also introduced a second variable about trust in the members of the association.

I have estimated a logistic regression model in which the dependent variable is trust in the members of the association (value 0 = do not trust, value 1 = trust). The independent variables include the type of associative organization (horizontal or vertical), as well as three control variables: education, income, and age. The variable of associative organization is a categorical one (value 0 = membership in vertical organizations, value 1 = membership in horizontal organizations). The results of the model are shown in table 4.1.

The results do not contradict the theoretical hypothesis. The type of organization has an impact on particularized trust. In particular, members of horizontal associations are more likely to trust their comembers than members of vertical ones. It seems, thus, that information and power asymmetries are a real obstacle for the development of relations of trust between the members of associations characterized by lack of accountability. The three control variables are also significant: elder and more affluent people tend to trust their fellow members more and, perhaps surprisingly, more educated people tend to trust less.

The relationship between type of association and trust in comembers can be seen more clearly in figure 4.2, which shows the predicted

Table 4.1. Logistic regression. Horizontal associations vs. vertical and particularized trust

Variables	Coefficients
Horizontal associations	1.177★★★
	(0.281)
Education	−0.234★★
	(0.099)
Income	0.137★★
	(0.068)
Age	0.016★
	(0.010)
Constant	−0.029
	(0.726)
Percentage of predicted cases	83.3%

Notes: Standard errors between brackets. ★★★ Significant at 99 percent. ★★ Significant at 95 percent. ★ Significant at 90 percent. The category of reference for voluntary associations is membership of vertical associations.

Source: Barómetro de opinión pública de Andalucía—2000 (IESAA/CSIC).

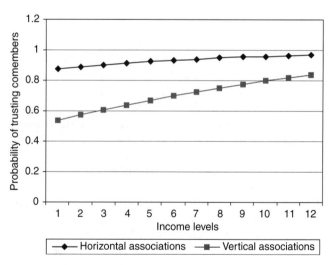

Figure 4.2 Type of associational organization and particularized trust (predicted probabilities)

probabilities of trusting fellow members. As can be seen, for all the income levels (1 being the lowest income level and 12 the highest), the probability of trusting in comembers is higher in horizontal associations than in vertical ones. In particular, this probability is 20–40 percent higher in horizontal associations than in vertical ones.

Another interesting and nonexpected result has to do with the impact of income in the probability of trusting the comembers of the associations. As we can see, the impact of the type of association on the probability of trusting comembers is especially strong for the lowest income level. As income increases, so does the probability of trusting comembers, and the differences between types of association in the generation of particularized trust decreases. For the highest income level, the impact of the type of associations on particularized trust is very small. This has probably to do with the effect of level of resources on trust. People with more resources (e.g., in terms of money) tend to be less risk-averse, because the potential losses if they place their trust erroneously are lower.

In the light of these results, it seems clear that there are good reasons to maintain that horizontal associations provide more favorable settings than vertical ones for the development of particularized trust.

To summarize the conclusions of this chapter, the creation of social capital as a by-product of other activities seems, therefore, a robust enough explanation in the case of particularized trust. Nevertheless, the information obtained from other people as a by-product of participation in social networks can often be misleading, or can be disregarded for various reasons. One curious example of this is the adaptation of beliefs to the feasible set of the decider. However, it is obvious that in many cases that information could be an adequate source of expectations about the other's behavior. In any event, as noted in chapter 3, this does not explain the differences in social capital among different communities. If particularized trust is simply a by-product of participation in associations, it is not very clear why there are more relations of trust in some communities than in others. In seeking to provide an answer to this question, I now consider social or generalized trust. As we already know, social trust poses a number of much more complex problems. In this case, expectations are a little more hazardous as they involve trust in unknown people. Can these sorts of expectations be by-products of other activities? In chapter 5, I consider the extent to which social trust can be created as a by-product of a particular activity, participation in associations, as well as proposing some alternative ways in which social trust can be created.

CHAPTER FIVE

The Creation of Social Trust

The literature on social capital, especially in political science, attaches great importance to social or generalized trust. Some authors consider that the notion of social trust represents the greatest contribution of the social capital school to the political culture research paradigm (Stolle, 2000). Social trust seems to be very important for the social capital research program, because many of the positive externalities associated with social capital are largely linked to the presence of social trust. The associations in Putnam's civic Italy make democracy work because they create social trust, trust in unknown people. Mothers can let their children play in the streets of Jerusalem because, unlike in Detroit, they believe that their neighbors, even if unknown, are trustworthy people (Coleman, 1990: 303).[1] In this chapter, I deal with the problems of the creation of social trust and propose different means of creating this particular expectation about unknown people's trustworthiness. However, before beginning the analysis of the formation of social trust, it would be convenient to remember in which sense social trust is related to social capital. As we have seen in chapter 2, trust is not in itself social capital. Social capital is the information derived from the membership in social networks, like a voluntary association, and the obligations of reciprocity derived from relations of trust. In chapter 2, I presented two mechanisms that linked trust to obligations of reciprocity: self-esteem and reputation. As we have seen, the trustee could want to keep the trust placed on her because she wants to maintain a certain reputation. The reputation of trustworthiness can be a source of future rents. For example, a woman with a reputation of being trustworthy can exchange commodities or other objects with other persons in the future. That is, reputation of trustworthiness pays in the future. However, in the case of social trust, the arguments presented in chapter 2 are opened at least to two objections. First, it is not clear why someone would like to seek a reputation of trust-worthiness with an unknown person. Why not simply get the money and run, given that the probability of another exchange with that unknown person in the future is highly unlikely? An answer to this objection is that, when deciding if being trustworthy with the unknown person who has entrusted you with something, you have to take into account not only that person but also other people from your own network of relationships that could change their expectations about your trustworthiness if they see you cheating that poor stranger. Although I depict in this chapter the social trust game as a two-player game (not taking into account nature's moves), it could actually be understood implicitly as a three-player game. When the trustee decides to cooperate or not with the truster, she has also to take into account the effects of her decision on her friends, work-mates, or, say, comembers of an association's expectations about her trust-worthiness. You can consider these exchanges as signals sent to a third player about your trustworthiness. Nevertheless, this argument is opened to a second objection. Why keep the trust placed on you by this unknown person if that third player is not seeing you? Suppose you live in a neigh-borhood at the outskirts of a big city and you happened to be walking in one the downtown's main streets, near the royal palace. A Japanese tourist asks you to take a photograph of him with his wife near the palace. He gives you his camera and goes back with his wife close to the palace. You have always wanted a camera like that (it's Japanese technology, after all) and you are sure that the tourist couple cannot reach you if you decide to steal the camera. Further suppose that the local police do not care much about these minor robberies, so the probability of being detained is zero. Moreover, given that your neighborhood's football team is play-ing a game with his main rival, the probability of one of your neighbors admiring the neoclassical architecture of the palace is close to zero. Why not simply steal the camera? There are two possible explanations, on which the Japanese tourist could have relied on one of them (or perhaps both) when making his expectation about your trustworthiness. First, you may think that there is a slight probability of being observed by one of your neighbors. One of the assumptions in this example was that this probability is extremely low. Nevertheless, why assume this risk, even if it is so small? Consider it from a rational perspective. If you decide to steal the camera, the probability of success is nearly 1, given that you are faster than the Japanese tourists and there is no police at sight. You like this type of camera very much and you love to take photographs, so the payoffs are considerable. Now consider the costs. One of them is the cost of being detained by the police. Assuming for convenience that the probability of detention is 0, your costs regarding this are therefore also 0. The other cost implies the loss of your reputation if you are observed by one of your neighbors. As we have seen, the probability of being observed is rather low, say, for example, 0.01. However, the costs you suffer if you are observed in terms of loss of reputation can be very high. If you have a reputation of trustworthiness, no doubt it will be completely destroyed if your acquaintances know what you have done to these foreigners who so kindly come to your country to admire its past artistic glories. If you do not have such a reputation, this single act will preclude you to obtain it in the future. Moreover, as I have said before, a reputation of trustworthiness is very useful for futures exchanges with other people. If you do not have it, these future exchanges will not take place. Given these parameters, it could be the same that, even though the probability of being observed by one of your acquaintances is rather low, the expected benefits of stealing the camera were surpassed by the expected costs.

That second explanation for not stealing the camera has to do with the second mechanism that linked trust and obligations of reciprocity in chapter 2. This second mechanism was self-esteem. As I have said in chapter 2, self-esteem is one of the most valuable goods, so you should have an interest in keeping it. Suppose that your self-image is that of a trustworthy person. Then, if you decide to steal the camera, inevitably this self-image will be damaged. Even though you love to take photographs and even though you like this type of camera so much that the expected benefits of stealing it surpass the expected costs in the terms presented earlier, you may decide not to steal it because it is costly to you in terms of the damage it inflicts on your self-image as a trustworthy person. However, it is true that this argument is more difficult to sustain in the case of social trust. It is conceivable that you decide not to steal the camera just because this would hurt your self-esteem but how would the truster—in this example, the Japanese tourist—know whether you have a self-image of a trustworthy person or not? In chapter 2, I proposed an example about how self-esteem could generate trustworthiness. This example was about Napoleon III and Cavour's meeting in Plombières to discuss Italy's future. In this example, Cavour counted on Napoleon's self-image as a revolutionary to obtain his support for a "liberation" war against Austria. However, in this case Napoleon's self-image was a sort of "common knowledge." In the example we are discussing here, our tourist does not have any idea about the other person's self-image. Of course, he could rely on some external signals about it: how he is dressed, or what gestures he makes, or similar information, to try to figure out what kind of person he is dealing with. However, given his basic lack of knowledge about the other person's self-image, it does not seem very promising to trust in someone you do not know just because you think that there is a certain probability (about which you do not know either) of this person having the self-image of trustworthiness. So, self-esteem is a mechanism scarcely applicable to the case of social trust. The tourist of our story could rely, nevertheless, on a reputational mechanism to evaluate the probability that the person to which he entrusts his camera will not cheat him.

The analysis of social trust is related to social capital, then, through its connection with obligations of reciprocity. This connection is mediated mainly through the operation of a reputational mechanism.

Once we have analyzed in what sense the analysis of social trust is related to the social capital research agenda, I deal specifically with the sources of social trust, the different ways of creating social trust. As we saw in chapter 3, social trust shares some features with public goods. In particular, it is a kind of trust that is very susceptible to opportunistic behavior. The mystery about social trust is that, if you do not have information about the other player, there is no good basis to know if he is trustworthy.[2] If this is the case, why trust? Obviously, if both players are opportunists, there are no reasons to trust. Kreps's "trust game" (1990) is relevant here, a game that is in fact a variant of the classic one-shot prisoner's dilemma. Figure 5.1 is a diagram of this game in extensive form.

The outcome of this trust game is that A will not trust B. And, in fact, Kreps's trust game is benevolent with respect to at least one of the two players. Note in figure 5.1 that, although B is unfortunately an

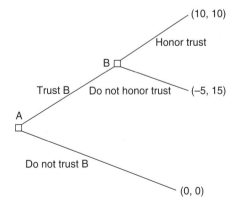

Figure 5.1 The trust game (Kreps, 1990: 100)

opportunist, the payoff structure of A is that of a more sympathetic guy: his first preference is to trust B if B is trustworthy. Kreps's trust game is a unilateral version of the prisoner's dilemma, with asymmetric payoffs. To better understand the logic behind this game, imagine that A is looking for a used car, and he hopes that the car bought from "honest B" is not a pile of junk. That is, his first preference is to trust B if he is trustworthy. The situation changes if we respect the traditional assumption of the prisoner's dilemma, in which both players are opportunists. The extensive form of the trust game in the classic prisoner's dilemma is depicted in figure 5.2. In this case the trust game is rather different. Now, unlike the game in figure 5.1, it is not a game in which one player places trust in another, and the latter has to decide whether or not to honor that trust, but a system of trust in which both players are at the same time truster and trustee. In this case, both players are opportunistic, that is, both want to cheat the other. The outcome is mutual distrust.

Both in Kreps's trust game and in the traditional version of the prisoner's dilemma, this outcome can be avoided if the game is iterated ad infinitum. In an example in which the trust game is iterated infinitely, or, more realistically, if neither A nor B know when the final play will be, the outcome can be that both players trust each other. An especially promising strategy in order to reach a cooperative equilibrium in the iterated trust game is tit-for-tat: "trust in the first round, and then do like

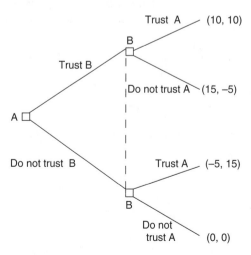

Figure 5.2   The trust game as a classical prisoner's dilemma

the other player in the previous round" (Axelrod, 1984). If both players choose tit-for-tat, the outcome of the game is that A and B trust, in the case of the prisoner's dilemma as a conventional prisoner's dilemma, or B honors A's trust, as in the case of Kreps's trust game.

Of course, a situation in which tit-for-tat is an equilibrium is just one of the many possible outcomes of the prisoner's dilemma super-game. An additional problem with this solution is that it is very unlikely to apply in the real world: generally speaking, cooperation is difficult to maintain if the game is not repeated (or there is a final game), if the other players do not have full information about each other, if there are a large number of players, or if players do not attach sufficient value to the future. In the case of impersonal interactions, these necessary conditions are rarely met (North, 1990: 12–13; Elster, 1985: 360–361). In any event, if a cooperative outcome is reached, this outcome would be nearer to particularized trust than to social trust. Through the iteration of the game, each player learns what he can expect from the other, and if it is worth carrying on playing tit-for-tat, or changing to a strategy in which, when the other player breaks trust, the first player never trusts him again.

In the case of social trust, the situation is somewhat different. Social trust is trust in unknown people. In this case, it seems useful to think in terms of a one-shot game, rather than on an iterated one. In iterated games, we are dealing with a different kind of game, relating to, as I have said, particularized trust.

Note that Kreps's is a perfect, certain, and complete information game. We can solve it very easily by backward induction. Moreover, player A's two moves, to trust or not to trust, are equal to cooperation or noncooperation. That is, this game does not capture the notion of trust as an expectation about the preferences of the other. The alternative is the social trust game shown in figure 5.3. In this game, player A's and player B's moves are different to those of Kreps's game. Trust and honor trust have been substituted by "cooperate," while distrust or not honor trust have been substituted by "defect." Further additions are probabilities θ and $1 - \theta$. These probabilities capture player A's expectations about B's trustworthiness. Player A has the same role as in Kreps's game. He is not opportunistic: his first preference is to cooperate with B if B is trustworthy. This outcome brings a payoff of b to player A. His second preference is defect B, an action that leads to the *status quo ante*. His last preference is to cooperate with B and be cheated by him. In this case, A will have a cost denoted by $-c$. The order of his payoffs is, therefore, $b > 0 > -c$. The biggest difference with Kreps's trust game is that, in the game shown in figure 5.2, there can be two different types of player B.

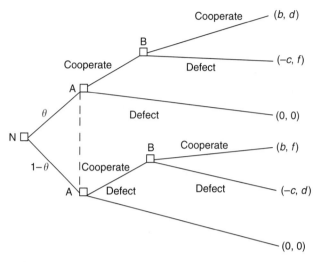

Figure 5.3   The social trust game

In the higher branches of the decision tree, B is trustworthy. In the lower branches, we find a player who is not very trustworthy. The difference between both types of B is reflected in their payoffs. A trustworthy B will obtain his maximum payoff (d) when he decides to honor A's cooperative mode. However, if B is an opportunist, he will obtain the higher utility by cheating player A. The second preference for a trustworthy B is that A does not cooperate with him. He will prefer that to cheating player A. Therefore, the order of his payoff is: $d > 0 > f$. The second preference of an opportunistic B will be that A does not cooperate with him. It is the same second preference as that of a trustworthy B, but for difference reasons. The opportunistic B will prefer not to establish a cooperative relation with A, in order to not assume the costs of this relation. His last preference then, is to honor A's cooperative move. The order of his payoff will be, therefore, $d > f > 0$. Player A must decide what type of B he is dealing with. Being a social truster, player A will assign a probability of $\theta > c/b + c$ of B being trustworthy, and, therefore, will cooperate with him.

Having determined the structure of social trust, we are still left with the question about the origins of these expectations. How is social trust created? In other words, how does player A form his subjective expectations (θ) about player B's trustworthiness?

As we have seen earlier, the first response to this question in the social capital literature is that social trust is created as a by-product of other activities, especially participation in associations. Unfortunately, this answer lacks micro-level foundations. The mechanisms that link social trust to participation in associations are generally not identified or, if they are, they tend to be weak and trivial. In the following sections of this chapter, I suggest various mechanisms for this relation. I will then move on to explore the creation of social trust using signs. Finally, in chapter 6, I analyze the role of the State in the generation of trust in unknown people.

The Creation of Social Trust as a By-Product of Other Activities

The creation of forms of social capital as a by-product of other activities is, as we have seen, an idea advanced by James Coleman (1990). In the case of social trust, that activity is often considered to be participation in associations. In *Making Democracy Work*, Robert Putnam (1993a) maintained that one of the ways to transform particularized trust into social trust was through participation in networks of civic engagement. These networks do not only include political associations but all kinds of voluntary associations, from bird-watching societies to football clubs. In this way Putnam expresses here Tocqueville's idea about the role of civil associations in "enhancing the heart and developing human spirit" (Tocqueville, 1996: 98). The problem with this source of social trust is that the mechanism linking participation in these types of associations and trust in nonmembers of the association is not very clear (Levi, 1996a: 47–48). That is, we do not know why a member of a football club, simply by the mere fact of being a member, will have a stronger predisposition to trust unknown people. I suggest the following five arguments should be considered:

1. The first concerns individuals' perception of the "type" of the rest of the population. A person trusts unknown people because he has had good experiences with comembers of his association and considers that these comembers are a representative sample of society at large.
2. The second argument considers participation in associations to be a way of learning to identify the tell-tale signs of properties inherent to trustworthy people.
3. The third considers the effects of deliberation within associations on the participants' beliefs about unknown people.
4. The fourth argument is a derivation of the third. It states that the effects of deliberation tend to vary in accordance with the aim of the association.
5. The fifth considers that the shape and number of an individual's social networks affects the development of trust in unknown people.

The first argument can occasionally be found in the social capital literature. It posits that people generalize from the expectations of trust developed within their associations because they consider that their comembers are representative of society at large. For example, if someone has had good experiences with members of his association, he will tend to think that people in general are trustworthy. Such positive expectation about people's trustworthiness will be stronger if the association is heterogeneous in terms of, for example, ideology, ethnicity, or social origins (Stolle and Rochon, 1998: 49; see also Blau, 1977: 36). That is, that development of social trust is easier in what Putnam calls "bridging" networks (2000: 22–23). In any event, such beliefs about the behavior of others are hardly rational.[3] Members of an association are clearly not a representative sample of human beings, and, in that sense, the extrapolation of their behavior to unknown people would not seem to be justified. If the sample is very big, it could be representative of the population under certain circumstances. However, this is not true of small samples, as is the case of most associations, which are, moreover, not random. Although a perfectly rational individual cannot believe that his association is a representative sample of society, things may look different if we relax the assumptions and introduce the notion of bounded rationality. Bounded rationality refers to the computational capacity of humans, or to the amount of information they can plausibly collate, for example, about other agents' strategies. This is combined with the complexity of the environment to explain the subjective perceptions of reality by humans (Williamson, 1985: 45–46; North, 1990: 25). Boundedly rational people therefore, are faced with uncertainty about unknown people's preferences, they face relatively high costs to gather and process information about those preferences, and it is fairly reasonable to believe that the problem of the representativeness of the sample is sufficiently complex for them to make mistakes. How can people in these circumstances form their expectations? One solution is to use some kind of heuristic, such as: "If the comembers of my association are trustworthy, I consider unknown people trustworthy." Participation in associations, therefore, can provide people with a tool to judge whether unknown people are trustworthy or not, and, in this sense, can promote the development of social trust. Cognitive psychology provides evidence to support this argument. A number of experiments carried out by cognitive psychologists have shown that people have strong intuitions (wrong most of the time), about random samples. In general, people think that samples, whatever their size, are very similar to each other and to the population. They also tend to think that sampling is a "self-correcting" process, so a deviation in one direction is compensated by a similar deviation in the opposite direction. This is what Tversky and Kahneman (1986) call "the law of small numbers": the law of big numbers also applies to small numbers, so the conclusions drawn from small samples are confirmed.

The second argument maintains that participation in associations is a way of learning how to read signals associated with trustworthiness. If we have developed relations of trust with the members of a group, or if we know some characteristics of the culture, traditions, or values of that group, then we can generalize that trust to people with an external sign of belonging to that group. This group may, for example, be an ethnic community (Bacharach and Gambetta, 1997; Offe, 1999: 63; Hardin, 1995; Blackburn, 1998) or an "imagined community" such as a nation (Whiteley, 1999: 31; Messick and Kramer, 2001: 102) or the fatherland (Hollis, 1998: 153–154). In this case, the way to reduce transaction costs is to associate certain visible traits (e.g., a form of dress or skin color) with certain characteristics (e.g., honesty) considered relevant to judge someone's trustworthiness (what Bacharach and Gambetta (2001) call "trust warranting properties"). In this sense, participation in networks would constitute a way of learning traits associated with trustworthiness that also serve to form expectations about the trustworthiness of unknown people. This is, therefore, the anteroom of Bacharach and Gambetta's (2001) "trust in signs," the way of learning what signs are linked to "trust-warranting properties," such as honesty. This way of learning about the "type" of trustworthy people is slightly different to Yamagishi's definition of social trust as a form of "social intelligence" (Yamagishi, 2001). According to Yamagishi, social trusters are people who, faced with high opportunity costs and high levels of social uncertainty, make big investments in cognitive resources, such as for example, attention and memory. Social trusters, in this account, take risks to learn more about other people's trustworthiness. In my account, social trusters trust unknown people because they have learnt inside their associations what signs are linked to trustworthiness. They face social uncertainty too, but the subjective probabilities they form about other people's trustworthiness are better founded thanks to their learning process within their associations. One objection to this mechanism is that it does not lead necessarily to social trust. It only led trust in those stranger that have certain characteristics that the individual associated to trustworthiness. These characteristics could be very few, and so the learning process of them inside the association could lead to more or less general distrust instead of general trust. Nevertheless, the point of this second argument is that people will be more self-confident in their expectations about other people's trustworthiness, and this will make them more open to trust in unknown people.

The third causal link between participation in associations and social trust consists of the way in which participation in associations can transform the beliefs of the participant through deliberation. This is the "republican" argument about the creation of social capital as a by-product of participation in associations. We saw in chapter 2 that deliberation in the form of discussion within associations can provide individuals with resources of social capital in the form of information. The present argument affirms that deliberation can also lead to a transformation in their preferences and beliefs.

The belief in the power of deliberation is, according to Cass Sunstein, one of the contributions of the Founders of the American Republic to the republican tradition (although it can be claimed that deliberation is a crucial component of the republican political system even from ancient Athens). The republican belief in deliberation assumes that actors must keep a critical distance from their desires and prevalent practices, subjecting them to scrutiny and revision (Sunstein, 1988: 1548–1549). In the republican literature we can find at least two strategies to argue that deliberation can lead to a transformation of preferences toward the common good. The first of these strategies relates to the structure of the deliberative process. The second involves the actors that participate in that process. This second strategy is of less interest for our discussion. It sustains that deliberation can lead toward the common good because participants have certain characteristics. These characteristics are, according to John Rawls (1995: 247), the realization of their two moral capacities—the capacity for a sense of justice and the capacity for a conception of good—and the desire to be fully cooperative members of society throughout their lives. Moreover, these people share a common human reason, similar powers of thought and judgment, and a capacity to draw inferences, weigh evidence, and compare and contrast competing ideas. These characteristics are similar to those of a virtuous citizen. This strategy is not very attractive for our purposes because it does not claim that civic virtue is the outcome of the deliberative process, but a prerequisite for it.

The first republican strategy claims that certain characteristics of the deliberative process can lead to a change of preferences. One of these characteristics could be the rules of the deliberative process. It is often argued that if deliberation is public, there is a pressure to abstain from egoistic arguments (Elster, 1993b: 183, 1995: 390). It is argued that participants do not wish to be seen as egoists, because that would be embarrassing (Fearon, 1998: 54). Another possible mechanism to explain why the participants in a deliberative process generally justify their points of view in terms of the common good is the psychological mechanism of reduction of cognitive dissonance: individuals tend to make what they think coincide with what they do, to reduce dissonance (Elster, 1987: 113). Another feature of deliberation that could lead to a change of preference is the revelation of private information (Fearon, 1998: 46; Gambetta, 1998: 22). Some participants may reconsider their preferences after taking into account new information. All three effects of deliberation can be related to the creation of social trust. First, public discussion leads people to present their arguments in terms of the common good, in order that people do not get embarrassed. The second effect then comes into play: to reduce dissonance by people matching what they think with what they do. If that were the case, presenting preferences in terms of the common good can lead to thinking in terms of the common good. The third effect, the collection of information about other participants, is independent of the other two. An example might illustrate how these effects of deliberation can relate to social trust. This example comes from James Fishkin and Robert Luskin's (2000: 25) "deliberative polls." At the beginning of one of these polls, an 84-year-old conservative white man from Arizona questioned whether one of his fellow group members, an African American woman on welfare from New York really had a family, on the ground that, in his opinion, a family required a mother, a father, and children. At the end of the weekend, he apologized to her and recognized that he was wrong. In this example two mechanisms may be in operation. The white conservative may change his beliefs about the African American woman on welfare (or perhaps, about New Yorkers) because he has had to refrain from making excessively unfriendly remarks about African Americans, in order to avoid embarrassment. Or he could simply have learnt more about African American women and begun to think that, after all, they are not untrustworthy.

Do these effects of deliberation on the participants' beliefs occur to the same degree in all type of associations? Yes, according to Putnam.[4] Other authors, such as Stolle and Rochon (1998), have shown that different types of associations have diverse implications for the generation of social trust. They found that cultural and community associations are strongly linked to generalized trust. In chapter 4, I advanced the idea that certain associations—those with a more democratic organization—are especially prone to deliberation. In this section, I briefly analyze the effects of the objectives of the association on deliberation, distinguishing between civil and political associations. This is the fourth mechanism of the relation between participation in associations and the development of social trust. This distinction is taken from Tocqueville, and is related to the association's objectives. According to Tocqueville (although on this issue, as on some others, *Democracy in America* is not always consistent) the development of political associations is easier than the development of civil associations. On the one hand, participation in civil associations is more costly: in most of them, members have to risk some of their money (it seems that Tocqueville was thinking about commercial or industrial associations). On the other hand, the benefits of associations seem higher in political life than in civic life. In civic life men are considered more autonomous, whereas in political life the need to cooperate to attain common objectives is more obvious (Tocqueville, 1996: 102–107). In Tocqueville's account, civil associations seem to be those formed to obtain a private good, whereas public associations are constructed for the attainment of a collective good, which in certain cases may also be a public good. While deliberation as discussion can take place in both types of association, from the point of view of deliberation as a way of developing social trust, political associations seem more interesting. This, at least, appears to be the case if we consider the content of discussion in both types of association. Some of the effects of deliberation, such as the revelation of private information or the overcoming of bounded rationality (Fearon, 1998) can take place both in political and civil associations. However, the transformation of beliefs into social trust seems more likely if the content of the discussion is political. This is due to two of the mechanisms noted earlier: the formulation of preferences in terms of the common good due to group pressure, and changes of preferences and beliefs in accordance with public formulation in order to reduce dissonance. My point is that in political associations, the pressures to formulate preferences and beliefs in terms of the common good encompasses not just the common good of the members of the association, but, by the very nature of the association, the common good of the community at large.

The fifth argument about the relation between participation in associations and the generation of social trust affirms that the former can also promote trust in nonmembers because the potential losses to the truster, in the event of the trustee not being trustworthy, are lower if the truster can rely on his social networks. If I am a member of various associations, and I have developed relations of particularized trust, I can trust an unknown individual, even if I do not know his type, because I can compensate for the potential losses of being cheated by relying on my social networks. More resources in terms of association membership then, clearly promote cooperation because it decreases the ratio between potential losses and potential gains. According to Coleman, an individual will trust (cooperate) if $pG > (1 - p)L$, that is, when $p/1 - p > L/G$, p = the probability of the trustee being trustworthy, L = potential losses, G = potential gains (Coleman, 1990: 99). Membership of a social network can reduce the ratio L/G in two ways. In figure 5.4, on the one hand, it can be argued that the losses for A of being cheated by E if he places trust in him will be perceived as potentially lower in this case because A can rely on B and D to reduce his losses. This argument is simply that an individual with more resources will suffer comparatively lower losses than an individual with less resources, and, therefore, he will tend to trust more, *ceteris paribus* (an individual with a lot of resources can, in spite of everything, be extremely distrustful due, e.g., to a low value of variable p in the equation). Given that social capital is a resource, this argument is also applicable in this case. A somewhat different argument relates the possession of social networks to other variables in the equation, in this case G, the potential gains. Returning to figure 5.4, if E responds favorably to the trust placed in him by A, this implies a gain for A. He adds E to his network of friends, and, therefore, he acquires potential resources of social capital to mobilize in the future. Now, let us suppose that A acquires various more relations through his membership of new social networks, or because his original network has expanded enormously. With this increase in the number of friends, it might be thought that the marginal utility of each new friendship is lower, that is, that the advantages for A of increasing his number of friends become lower and lower. Compare this situation to the opposite, that of a solitary individual. An inhabitant of Hobbes's state of nature, where life is "solitary, poor, nasty, brutish and short" (Hobbes, 1992: 108) will value a friend more highly. That is, if for A the variable G has a low value, for a solitary individual, the value of G is much higher. However, my point is not that participation in social networks enhances cooperation because

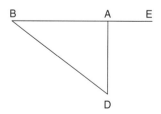

Figure 5.4   Social network and social trust

it reduces the ratio L/G, but that it enhances cooperation because it increases the ratio $p/1 - p$, that is, because it increases social trust. Expectations about unknown people's trustworthiness can change through a process of "rationalization of hope" (a process referred to in chapter 4). Rationalization of hope is an unconscious impulse and, although it cannot be causally rooted on the available information, it can at least be supported by that information. This process should especially affect people with small resources of social capital. As I have said, in this case the potential benefits (G) of engaging in a new relation are very high, and this makes the decision to cooperate with unknown people more likely. How could a process of rationalization of hope operate in this context? People could not have enough information to assess another person's trustworthiness. However, given that for people with few relations the benefits of engaging in a new one could be very high, they could point to some apparently irrelevant or minor evidence to update their beliefs about the other person's trustworthiness. Nevertheless, the costs of trusting untrustworthy individuals can be especially high in this case, given that there is nobody to rely on. In Thomas Hardy's classical novel *Tess of the D'Urbervilles*, the heroine trusts her cousin Alec, with the predictable outcome in a naturalist novel worthy of the name that she is seduced and gets pregnant. The outcome is all the more terrible because Tess has practically no friends to rely on and her family would be classified in any modern day social capital study as unstructured. In what sense are the losses experienced by Thomas Hardy's heroine especially serious? It could be in two senses. First, Tess's lack of social relations means that she will have difficult times. In fact, in the novel, Tess has to suffer the foreseeable embarrassment of being pregnant without being married in a nineteenth-century European peasant community. She has nearly nobody to rely on for consolation, for example. There is also a second sense in which the lack of social relations could make the trust that Tess mistakenly put on her cousin Alec especially costly. Lack of social relations means, to a certain extent, lack of what Yamagishi (2001) calls "social intelligence." This means that, if you are isolated, it is difficult for you to learn the signals that identify trustworthy people. Before her relation with her cousin, young Tess did not have enough social intelligence to distinguish trustworthy from untrustworthy people. Her sad experience makes matters worse, given that Tess will be compressively much more cautious in dealing with other people (in the novel, she finally marries Angel Clare, just to be miserably disappointed a second time, although for altogether different reasons: now she had basis to trust but is nonetheless disappointed).

Given that the losses experienced in these cases when there are no social networks on which to rely on can be especially serious, it might be the case that expectations have a positive shape to certain states of the world that I prefer to occur above certain states of the world that go against these expectations. The consequence, therefore, would be a higher expectation of p, that is, a higher probability of trusting unknown people, *ceteris paribus*.[5]

This outcome is rather paradoxical given the argument about the generation of social capital as a by-product of participation in associations. This argument, however, considers that the higher your resources of social capital, for example, because you participate in many associations, the lower the benefits of trusting unknown people. Actually, this outcome is not as unlikely as it may sound. We can in fact identify this idea in Putnam's concept that certain associations are self-sufficient and exclusive (Putnam, 2000: 22), although applied here to all kinds of associations. The idea I have just developed does not mean, however, that the greater the number of associations, the lower the amount of social capital. It implies that the marginal benefits of new personal relations decrease, and this should have an impact on the decision to trust in unknown people. We have here two contradictory conclusions. If it is supposed that membership of associations fosters trust in unknown people to the extent that the members of your association are considered a representative sample of society, it could be expected that the higher the number of associations, the greater the probability of trusting unknown people. Nevertheless, given that, beyond a certain point, the marginal benefits of trust in unknown people decrease beyond a certain point, it may be the case that, by belonging to many associations, your probability of trusting unknown people begins to decrease. The relation between the number of associations and the probability of trust in unknown people would take the form shown in figure 5.5.

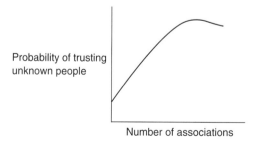

Figure 5.5   Number of associational memberships and trust

These then, are the five mechanisms that I consider are at work in the relationship between participation in associations and social trust. The central hypothesis behind all of them is that participation in associations fosters social trust. I will test this hypothesis in chapter 6, in which I present a simultaneous equation model of a virtuous circle of the creation of social capital. However, I test here two hypotheses derived from mechanisms 4 and 5 that are not relevant to the model of the virtuous circle. These hypotheses are the following:

> Hypothesis 1. The probability of developing social trust is greater inside political associations.
> Hypothesis 2. The larger the number of memberships of associations, the greater the probability of trusting unknown people until, that is, a point is reached where the probability of trusting unknown people begins to decrease.

Hypothesis 1

In order to test the first hypothesis, I have once again used the Barometer of Andalusian Public Opinion of 2000. I have estimated a logistic regression model in which the dependent variable is social trust (value 0 = do not trust unknown people, value 1 = trust). Among the independent variables, I have included one related to type of association. This variable is a categorical one (value 0 = membership of a civil association, value 1 = membership of a political association). The control variables are education, income, and age.

The results of the logistic regression are shown in table 5.1. These results do not contradict the theoretical hypothesis. The variable "political associations" is significant and the direction of the coefficient is correct. The probability of trusting unknown people is greater if the individual is a member of political associations than if he is a member of civil organizations. This relationship can more clearly be seen in figure 5.6, which shows the predicted probabilities of trusting unknown people by types of associational membership. The probability of trusting unknown people is between 8 and 15 percentage points higher, depending on income level, if the individual is a member of a political rather than a civil association. According to the arguments presented in this chapter, this could have to do with the content of the discussions inside both types of associations. In political associations, it is more likely that the discussion is referred to the common good of the wider community and not only to the interests of the members of the associations. This could contribute to the generation of positive beliefs about the nonmembers of the association's

Table 5.1 Logistic regression. Political associations vs. civil and social trust (Dependent var.: social trust)

Variables	Coefficients
Political associations	0.595★★
	(0.195)
Education	0.162★★
	(0.064)
Income	0.153★★
	(0.048)
Age	0.005
	(0.007)
Constant	−2.781★★★
	(0.495)
Percentage of predicted cases	69.5%

Notes: Standard errors in brackets. ★★★ Significant at 99 percent. ★★ Significant at 95 percent.

Source: *Barómetro de opinión pública de Andalucía—2000 (IESAA/CSIC).*

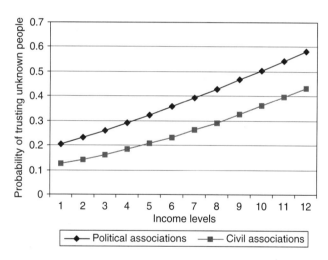

Figure 5.6 Type of association and social trust (predicted probabilities)

trustworthiness. Regarding the other variables in the model higher levels of education and income, as it was expected, increase social trust. We have already seen this effect, referred more concretely to income levels, in chapter 5, when we were analyzing the development of particularized trust inside different types of associations. Our conclusion there was that higher-income levels mean higher resources, less risk aversion and, thus, a higher probability of trusting the comembers of your association. This conclusion can be extended here to education and trust in unknown people.

Hypothesis 2

I have also used data from the Barometer of Andalusian Public Opinion of 2000 in order to test the second hypothesis. I have estimated a logistic regression model in which the dependent variable is again social trust (value 0 = do not trust unknown people, value 1 = trust). Among the independent variables, I have included three categorical variables relating to the number of associational memberships: membership of three associations, of two associations, and of one. In each of these variables, the category of reference is membership of four associations. That is, the coefficients of each of these variables tell us about how membership of one, two, or three associations affects trust in unknown people as compared to membership of four associations. The control variables are education and income.

The results of the model are shown in table 5.2. As can be seen, the variables relating to the number of associational memberships are not

Table 5.2 Logistic regression. Number of associations and social trust (dependent var.: social trust)

Variables	Coefficients
Membership to one association	−0.507
	(0.475)
Membership to two associations	−0.381
	(0.496)
Membership to three associations	0.365
	(0.535)
Education	0.125**
	(0.065)
Income	0.135**
	(0.050)
Constant	−1.773**
	(0.596)
Percentage of predicted cases	69.1%

Notes: Standard errors in brackets. ** Significant at 95 percent.

Source: *Barómetro de opinión pública de Andalucía-2000 (IESAA/CSIC)*.

significant. Nevertheless, the sign of the coefficients is interesting. It shows that the probability of trust in unknown people is lower if the individual is a member of one or two associations than if he is a member of four associations. But the most trusting individuals are the members of three associations. Although the coefficients are not significant, it is worth noting that their direction is consistent with the hypothesis tested: an increase in the number of associations is linked with higher levels of social trust, at least up to a certain point. Beyond this point, the probability of trusting unknown people begins to decrease. In figure 5.7, I have calculated the predicted probabilities. Although the coefficients are not significant, this figure clearly shows that the direction of those coefficients is as predicted in the hypothesis. This hypothesis stated that more resources in terms of relationships increase the probability of engaging in trust relations but, once a certain point is reached, this probability begins to decrease, given that the marginal utility of new relations decreases. For this reason, perhaps, membership of three associations is related to the maximum point in social trust and this relation decreases in the case of membership of four associations.

With this, I have completed my analysis of the causal mechanisms at work in the creation of social trust as a by-product of participation in associations. I turn now to the second source of social trust: signals as a source of expectations of trust about unknown people.

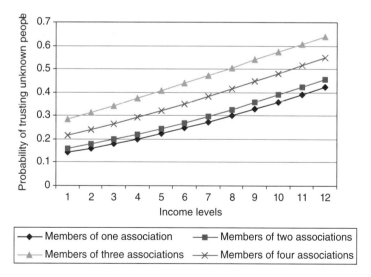

Figure 5.7 Number of associations and social trust (predicted probabilities)

Signals as a Source of Social Trust

In the previous discussion of the various mechanisms involved in the creation of social trust as a by-product of participation in associations, I mentioned that membership can be considered a way of learning signs associated with trustworthiness. In this section, I consider this topic from the opposite angle, that is, I discuss how people can induce other people to trust them by giving certain signals of trustworthiness.

The structure of this method of creating social trust can be seen in figure 5.8, which presents the game of trust as a signaling game. This signaling game, like the trust game in figure 5.3, is a game with imperfect and asymmetric information. In these kinds of games, all players have private information. The private information held by each player determines her type. As in the social trust game, one of the players, in this case player A,

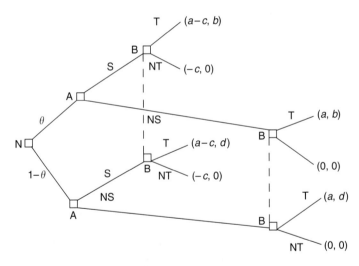

Figure 5.8   The trust game as a signaling game

Notes
Moves of player A:
S = send a signal
NS = do not send a signal
Moves of player B:
T = trust
NT = do not trust
θ = Probability of being trustworthy
$1 - \theta$ = probability of being untrustworthy

can be one of two types: trustworthy or opportunistic. However, in this case player A can communicate her private information through a signal to player B before player B's decision. In this case, the signal sent by player A enables player B to update her own expectations about A's trustworthiness. That is, an individual can consciously use external signals that she knows are associated with characteristics, such as honesty, that are considered typical of a trustworthy person. These are what Bacharach and Gambetta (2001) term "trust warranting properties," which induce trust. In Truman Capote's novel *In Cool Blood*, the two main characters decide to change their external appearances, to shave and put on new clothes before going out to pay with dud checks in various Kansas City shops. The victims of the fraud subsequently declared that the characters seemed trustworthy because they were smartly dressed and well-spoken. In *The Prince*, Machiavelli contends that citizens, who do not personally know their ruler, must base their trust on external signals and appearances, thus enabling the ruler to behave in an opportunistic way. For example, even though the State will benefit if the prince is parsimonious, in order to obtain power he is better advised to give (false) signals of generosity (Machiavelli, 1992: 85, 92). Of course, the sender of signals is not necessarily an opportunist. His intentions may be good, that is, to show another party that he is trustworthy when in fact he is.

In the game in figure 5.8, player A has two options: to send a signal to player B (S) or not to send it (NS). Sending a signal implies a cost, c, that affects the payoff of player A if he sends a signal. If B decides to trust him, he receives a payoff of a. If B decides not to trust him, he receives a 0 payoff. The ranking of his payoff is, therefore: $a > a - c > 0 > -c$, assuming that the benefits of obtaining B's trust are greater than the cost of sending a signal. Player B has two options: trust A (T) or not trust A (NT). He receives a payoff b if he trusts A and A is trustworthy, a payoff d if he trusts in an opportunistic A, and 0 if he decides not to trust. The order of his payoff is, therefore: $b > 0 > d$. In this game various equilibria can be reached. In one of them, player B trusts A because the signal he receives makes him update his prior information about player A's type. It is the following equilibrium: (S/Trustworthy, NS/Opportunistic; T, NT: 1, 0). That is, if player A is trustworthy, he sends a signal of trustworthiness. If he is an opportunist, he does not send the signal. If both types send signals, they do not provide player B with new information. In this case, a possible pooling equilibrium is: (S/Trustworthy, S/Opportunist; T, T: θ, 0) with $\theta > d/d - b$. Therefore, given the payoffs of the game in figure 5.8, only if player B's prior information about A's trustworthiness are higher than $d/d - b$, will he trust.

In the game in figure 5.8, player A can give signals that lead player B to trust him. Player B has prior information about A's trustworthiness. This prior knowledge can be higher or lower than $d/d - b$. Player A generates social trust, giving player B key information to update his prior knowledge in order to trust a stranger. Founding one's expectations on external signs may not be the best way of forming one's beliefs. In his work *Brutus*, Cicero considered that sometimes people use erroneous signals to judge politicians' personal characteristics. Wealth is clearly this type of signal: occasionally (although not always) people confuse virtue with opulence and wealth (Cicero, *Brutus*: 184–186). Returning to Machiavelli, he considered that the people did not have enough information about the politicians' personal characteristics, and, so, it was difficult to select virtuous agents. In the *Discorsi*, Machiavelli said that "the people judge in the elections according to the surest signals about the men's character" (Machiavelli, 1996: 396). He even concedes that these pieces of information about personal characteristics are a reasonable shortcut to select good agents (Machiavelli, 1996: 393). Nevertheless, as it is clear in some passages of *The Prince* and the *Discorsi*,[6] Machiavelli considered that the governors had a wide capacity of mimicking signals associated to "trust-warranting properties." In terms of the game of figure 5.8, he thought that the sending of signals was relatively cheap, and so a pooling equilibrium is the most likely result of the game.

Let me present now an example that illustrates this idea that trust in signs can be fruitfully analyzed from the supply side, that is, as a source of social trust. It is the case of the political entrepreneurs in Vietnam during the struggles against the French and the Americans.[7]

Traditional peasant communities in Vietnam were not characterized by high levels of trust. This may sound strange, given that it is usually assumed that small rural communities are especially likely to develop relations of trust. The overcoming of dilemmas of collective action in small peasant communities is a central point in Michael Taylor's work (Taylor, 1988). Taylor's declared aim was to add micro-foundations from rational choice theory to the arguments that Theda Skocpol makes in *States and Social Revolutions* about the revolutionary activity of peasant communities in France, Russia, and China.

Vietnamese villages were undoubtedly small communities, with between 300 and 1,000 inhabitants. Families were grouped into hamlets. Each village had a boss, a board of notables, and a system of ranks or orders that determined the social hierarchy. Most of the land (some three-quarters) was private property in the hands of peasant families. The remaining quarter was (at least in the provinces of Tonkin and Annam) common land, managed and controlled by the board of notables and the village boss. Vietnamese villages were riven by competing interests among their members, and, hence, by deep distrust that made it difficult to resolve numerous social dilemmas. Resources in the village were scarce, provoking competition and tension among peasants.

Distrust was mainly directed against the notables, the rich peasants who governed the village. This distrust, it should be noted, exemplifies the difficulties involved in creating relations of trust in vertical organizations. As we saw in chapter 4, one solution to this problem it to institute fixed institutional rules that clearly set down the proper behavior of each agent, and the punishments applicable in the event of misconduct. There were fixed institutional rules in Vietnamese villages. However, rather than representing credible commitments by the hierarchically superior villagers not to exploit poorer peasants, the rules merely confirmed the prevailing inequalities. The fixed rules assigned resources to peasants according to their rank in the village, which was determined by age, wealth, and formal education. Thus, the position of the notables was reinforced, as were their incentives to exploit poorer peasants. In fact, the notables used their privileged position to obtain further advantages over the peasants. The richest members of the village served on the board of notables, and, thus, they had access to the village list and the mandarin's roll. The number of peasants registered on the mandarin's roll determined the amount of taxes to be paid by the village. Thus, it was in the village's collective interest to have as few peasants as possible registered. However, the notables had an individual interest in being included on the roll, as registration meant access to the board of notables, the possibility of presenting suits in the courts, the power to ask for help from the mandarins, or to travel in safety out of the village. These benefits were used by the notables to reinforce their position. Moreover, even though theoretically only those registered on the mandarin's roll were liable to pay taxes, in practice all villagers were obliged to pay taxes, the total sum due being shared out equally among all the members of the village.

Distrust and envy were also generalized attitudes among poor peasants in Vietnamese villages. Given the scarcity of resources and the competition for them, peasants viewed life as a zero-sum game. Thus, they considered that noncooperation was their best strategy, since cooperation implied the risk of giving an advantage to one's neighbor. Trust was confined to certain horizontal relations, between members of the same family and friends. These limited relations of trust did not extend beyond the village: there was widespread distrust of strangers. That is, Vietnamese peasants were not characterized by strong expectations of generalized trust. Furthermore, distrust was predictably lower among the poorest peasants, because of their lack of resources. Accordingly, higher levels of trust characterized social relations in Cochinchine, the richest province in Vietnam.

Among the notables themselves distrust was also the rule. For example, in the decision-making process within the board decisions were taken by the unanimous vote of all the notables. This did not reflect consensus, but distrust. Unanimity implied that all of them had the power of veto over any decision that could damage their interests. In reality, when a notable could use whatever external influence he had to improve his situation with respect to the other notables, he would not hesitate to do so. During French rule, the village's chiefs used their relations with French authorities to undermine the power of the other notables.

Given this situation of generalized distrust among peasants and notables, on the one hand, and within each of these groups, on the other, it was very difficult to carry out public tasks requiring widespread cooperation. Nevertheless, there was a limited degree of cooperation. Small peasant associations did exist, such as those created to share the expenses of celebrating communal feasts, the cost of buying pigs, or the costs of religious ceremonies. In all these cases, the main source of cooperation was not relations of trust. Participation in most of these associations did not require high levels of trust. Their aim was the provision of not public, but private good. For example, associations for sharing the costs of buying pigs only benefited members of the association. Nonmembers had to assume themselves the costs of buying a new pig. Other associations were more clearly orientated toward the provision of public good. We can assume that religious feasts were a public good, given that the beneficiaries included all members of the village (including free-riders). In this case, the peasants' preferences were those of a coordination game, not a prisoner's dilemma. That is, an individual's first preference was full collaboration of all peasants, including himself, in the preparation of the feast. But if the others were not willing to cooperate, he would prefer not to cooperate. In this situation, expectations about the others could be crucial. However, as we know, Vietnamese villages were not characterized by the existence of widespread relations of trust. Thus, the solution to social dilemmas required investment in monitoring. Given that associations were small, monitoring costs were not very high, and so cooperation could be sustained. However, these costs would have been considerably lower if there had been widespread trust.

In this hostile setting for the development of relations of trust, political entrepreneurs began to operate during the period of French colonial rule. These political entrepreneurs belonged to different organizations: the Catholic Church, sects such as Cao Dai and Hoa Hoa, and the Communist Party. These political entrepreneurs played a crucial role in overcoming many of the collective-action problems faced by Vietnamese peasants. According to Popkin, they manipulated the information to convince the peasants that their contribution was crucial to the achievement of a certain aim, or, for example, they divided a global aim into smaller ones with critical thresholds.

Over and above the question of how political entrepreneurs overcame the collective-action problems found in Vietnamese villages, there remains a problem in Popkin's work with respect to how they first managed to win the support of the peasants. This is a serious dilemma, especially in communities characterized by distrust of strangers.

To solve this problem, political entrepreneurs used one of the strategies available to player A in the game in figure 5.8: they sent signals of trustworthiness. These signals had to prove to the peasants that they were trustworthy. If the signals worked, peasants would consider the political entrepreneur trustworthy.

What kind of signals did the political entrepreneurs send? One example is the use of the same language as the peasants. Many political entrepreneurs failed because they did not use that language. In villages in Tonkin and Annam province, the original Communist and Trotskyst political entrepreneurs, city dwellers educated in French schools in Vietnam itself, or even in Europe (whose knowledge of peasant life was in many cases confined to what they had read in Vietnamese translations of French books), failed in their attempts to recruit peasants to their struggle. In contrast, from the very beginning Catholic priests talked to the peasants in their own language, using the same vocabulary and expressions. This strongly favored communication and also acted as a signal. Later, however, a new style of Communist militant emerged who were able to win the peasants' trust by "singing stories," a way of communicating news that was very familiar to peasants. A story told by the cadres of Nghe-Tinh's Soviet in 1930–31 constitutes a striking example of this, as under the title of "The Advice of a Wife to Her Husband to Make the Revolution," the story recounted Marx's adventures in Paris during the 1848 revolution (Woodside, 1976: 181). Another signal that could have been favorably interpreted by peasants was the celibacy practiced by Catholic priests. The equivalent signal sent by the members of the Cao-Dai sect and the Communist militants was their asceticism. Both wore clothes that were not very different to those of the poor peasants. Ho Chi Minh himself, who came from a leading family of the Vietnamese Confucian *intelligentsia*, spoke to the people of various villages of the Nung region in summer 1941, dressed as a peasant (Woodside, 1976: 222).

In many cases, signals sent by political entrepreneurs were intentional, in line with the strategy outlined in the game in figure 5.8. In the case of the Catholic priests, while celibacy cannot strictly be seen as a conscious signal, their use of the peasants' expressions and vocabulary certainly can. Equally, wearing peasant-style clothes and eating like the poor were conscious signals sent by Communist political entrepreneurs to prove their trustworthiness. Sometimes, these signals were taught to future political entrepreneurs. One example of this comes from the "Tonkin's Free School," an institution created in Hanoi in 1907 by the local elite to spread nationalists ideas among the peasants. The young students, who were usually mandarin's sons, were advised that to win the support of the peasantry they ought "to leave broad sleeves and loose clothes and to wear peasants' clothes" (Woodside, 1976: 41). These signals provided peasants with information about specific traits of the political entrepreneurs. In particular, the austere lifestyle cultivated by political entrepreneurs could be interpreted by Vietnamese peasants as a reflection of non-egoistic preferences. The political entrepreneurs' proclamations, for example, that their goal was to improve the peasants' living conditions rather than favor their own self-interest, might seem more credible if the austerity practiced by Communist and Cao-Dai activists was interpreted as a signal of their altruistic preferences.

In this case, therefore, political entrepreneurs worked consciously to create expectations of social trust among peasants. Signals (in many cases at least) were sent intentionally, and, after receiving them, peasants updated their prior beliefs about the political entrepreneur's trustworthiness. Their prior beliefs depended on many factors, such as, for example, the generalization to unknown people of the expectations of trust developed within the village. In the case of the Vietnamese village, this type of generalization process should have resulted in high levels of distrust of strangers (and that indeed was the case). The signals sent by political entrepreneurs made peasants modify their expectations in favor of trusting them. This updating of beliefs depended, of course, on the relative cost of the different signals sent by the political entrepreneurs. As we have seen, the probability of a separating equilibrium in the game of figure 5.8, a type of equilibrium in which just the trustworthy type sends the signal, depends much on the cost of the signal. As we have seen, for authors like Machiavelli, signals related to virtue are easily mimicked, so a pooling equilibrium is always the most probable result. However, in the example of Vietnam, there are obvious differences in terms of costs between simply dressing like a poor peasant and living like one. Peasants could rely on the relative costs of the signals to assess its credibility. Of course, from the peasant's point of view this way of updating beliefs was not very costly. This does not mean, however, that it was rational. According to Popkin (1991), the use of shortcuts of this kind to reduce the transaction costs involved in gathering and processing information is rational if it leads the agent to make the same decision that he would have reached if he had gathered all the relevant information. It is doubtful whether the use of external signals represented a rational shortcut for the Vietnamese peasants. However, from a supply-side perspective, that is, from the point of view of the political entrepreneurs, it was an efficient way of creating social trust.

Conclusions

In this chapter, I have presented various arguments as to how social trust can be created as a by-product of participation in associations, and how individuals can invest in the creation of trust by sending signals about their trustworthiness (or manipulating other signals when the sender is not really trustworthy). In the first case, I have put forward new mechanisms to explain the link between participation in associations and social trust. In the second, I have tried to formalize the idea and illustrate it. In chapter 6, I close the arguments in this book about the creation of social trust. I analyze the role of the State in the creation of social trust. This is an especially important topic, given that some of the clues to understand the difference in social capital between communities can be in the different actions undertaken by the State.

CHAPTER SIX

The Creation of Social Trust—the Role of the State

There is widespread belief in the literature that the role of the State in the creation and maintenance of social capital has been neglected. The key criticism to the most important study of social capital to date in this field, Robert Putnam's *Making Democracy Work*, is that—aside from its historical flaws—it is largely silent on the role of the State (Levi, 1993, 1996a; Tarrow, 1996; Morlino, 1995; Skocpol, 1996; Vallely, 1996; O'Neill, 1996; Berman, 1997). Putnam is not alone in neglecting the role of the State. Scholars working within the social capital paradigm have often assigned the State a negative role in the creation of this form of capital. It is significant that the only reference to the responsibility of the State for the decline of "civic America" is to be found in Putnam's *Bowling Alone*, where he argues that the State is one of the primary "suspects" responsible for the decline in social capital (281). Even if the State is finally acquit, it is significant that it was initially thought that "more State could be synonymous with less social capital." Nonetheless references to the role of the State in undermining social capital are, in fact, more common than statements to the contrary.[1]

Commenting on Putnam's analysis in *Making Democracy Work*, Boix and Posner argue that the historical difference in social capital between northern and southern Italy was due to the Norman State acting as an obstacle to the cooperation of the southern peasants (Boix and Posner, 1996). Anthony Padgen (1988) believes that the responsibility for the destruction of social capital in southern Italy lies with the Spanish viceroys. The Spaniards, through institutions such as the Inquisition and a policy of "*divide et impera*" among the local aristocracy, destroyed the relations of trust inside the Neapolitan society. Other authors have also stressed the negative impact of the modern State on social capital. Returning to the Italian case, it has been argued that the institutional reforms of the *Risorgimento* resulted in the destruction of the local networks of mutual help and public charity of the feudal era (Sabetti, 1996: 27–32). In general terms, the modern State has been seen as destroying spontaneous informal networks of interaction (Levi, 1996b: 8). In the case of twentieth-century Russia, it has been argued that the Soviet reforms of Stalin's period led to the destruction of all autonomous loci of social participation: colleges, sports, and voluntary associations were closed down and small towns were annihilated by collectivization. The Soviet regime has been seen as consciously setting out to destroy social capital (Nichols, 1996: 634–638), a charge that has also been made against other Communist countries' regimes, for example, Ceaucescu's Romania (Mondak and Gearing, 1998).

As has been pointed out by critics of the "neo-Tocquevillian" approach to the social capital research program (Foley and Edwards, 1998a),[2] lying behind the analysis that ascribes a minimal or negative role to the State is the idea that "civil society" is a sphere that is autonomous from the State, and that more State equals less civil society. For those working in the social capital research paradigm, this means that the State hinders the development of voluntary associations, or that associations created by the State generate less social capital because they lack spontaneity (Stolle and Rochon, 1999; Fukuyama, 1998: 18).

In this chapter, I challenge the view outlined earlier and suggest an alternative vision of the State's role in the creation of social capital. First, I consider the arguments that treat the State as an external agent in the resolution of collective-action dilemmas. I then develop a number of more specific ideas about how the State can facilitate the creation of various forms of social capital. Although most of this section focuses on the role of the State in creating social trust, some of the conclusions reached could equally well be applied to particularized trust. In particular, the role of the State in strengthening of the associative network can generate, as a by-product, increased social and particularized trust between members of associations.

External Solutions to the Dilemmas of Collective Action

As noted earlier, the creation of social capital often results in a social dilemma, due to the public-good features of social capital. How can this social dilemma be overcome?

A common solution to the social dilemmas derived from the existence of a public good is the adjudication of sanctions (positive or negative) by an external agent. The most common example of a centralized external solution is the State. This external agent offers the necessary incentives to prevent people free-riding, mainly in the form of negative sanctions for noncooperative behavior, but also through positive sanctions to promote cooperation. In this way, the intervention of this external agent resolves problems relating to public or common goods (Hardin, 1978: 314; Heilbroner, 1974).

This approach has some problems. The first derives from the restrictive nature of some of its assumptions, and more particularly, the implicit assumption that the external agent has full information about noncompliant behavior. If, however, only incomplete information is available about the strategies of the main actors (a fairly reasonable assumption), the administration of sanctions will be unsuccessful, and the outcome could be a noncooperative equilibrium (Ostrom, 1990: 11–12; Hollis, 1998: 32). A second weakness of this approach springs from a more fundamental problem. In fact, the presence of an authority that provides selective incentives for cooperation implies that another problem of collective action must already have been resolved (Elster, 1991: 56–57). I am referring here to a second-order collective-action problem: the sanctioning of noncooperative behavior itself poses a problem of collective action, since the effective sanction of such behavior has positive externalities (Coleman, 1990: 270–273).

I now move on to analyze in more detail the role of the State in creating social trust. Here I do not go into this second criticism of the role of the State as an external agent in the solution of dilemmas of collective action, as the discussion of that problem is not the aim of this chapter, which is to consider the influence of the State in the creation of social capital. First, I analyze how social trust can be directly created by the State. This analysis stresses the role of the State as a sanctioning agent that guarantees the fulfillment of agreements. Second, I analyze another, indirect way in which the State can create social trust: by favoring participation in associations. If we assume that participation in associations is related to the development of social trust, then if the State promotes this form of participation it should, indirectly, play a positive role in creating social capital.

The State as a Guarantor of Agreements

As we have already seen, social trust is a rather problematic form of social capital. It implies trust in unknown people, that is, in people whose trustworthiness is unknown (e.g., no information is available about their past behavior). If we are faced with uncertainty, the decision to trust will depend on sufficiently high expectations about the "type" of that unknown person.

So far, we have seen how specific expectations of social trust may be a by-product of participation in associations, or a result of updating prior beliefs after receiving a signal sent by the unknown person revealing that she is trustworthy. In this chapter, I analyze a third way of creating social trust which, for the first time, involves the State.

The State can favor the development of social trust by sanctioning those who do not honor trust placed in them. If we know that any non-compliance with an agreement will be sanctioned by the State, we will have greater expectations about other people's compliance. This is one of Margaret Levi's (1996b, 1997) arguments about the State's role in creating interpersonal trust. Figure 6.1 shows the same game of social trust depicted in figure 5.3, except for the incorporation of a State that applies sanctions to people who do not honor trust placed in them. It is similar to Elinor Ostrom's version of the prisoner's dilemma (1990: 10). In this case, the State imposes a sanction (s) when player B decides not to honor trust, a sanction that has a negative impact on his payoff. This sanction is sufficiently high for $f > d - s$. Whereas in the game of social trust, player A cooperated when $\theta > c/b + c$, in this case A cooperates when $b > 0$,

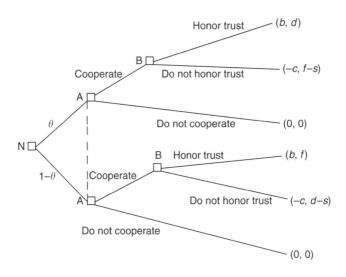

Figure 6.1   The game of social trust with a sanctioning State

that is, when there is a benefit, whatever its size, of trusting B if B is trustworthy. This is a much more favorable outcome in terms of the development of cooperation.

A problem with this solution is that, although the game shown in figure 6.1 assumes that player A does not have full information about the payoffs for player B, it is assumed that the State has full information about those who breach trust placed in him. If we assume that the State can make mistakes when applying sanctions, we will be in the game depicted in figure 6.2. In this game, once player B decides not to honor the trust placed in him, the State can apply a sanction. But, in this case, the State can be mistaken, and not apply the sanction. In the case of both types of player B, the opportunistic and the trustworthy, the State will sanction the nonfulfillment of agreements with probability β, and will not sanction them with probability $1 - \beta$. In this game, this is reflected in a move by Nature once player B decides not to honor the trust placed in him. The trustworthy B will always honor A's trust, given that $d > f > f - s$, and the opportunistic B will do the same when $\beta > (d - f)/s$. That is, he will honor the trust placed in him if the ratio between the difference between the payoff for being trustworthy and the payoff for cheating A and not being sanctioned, and the scale of the sanction, is lower than the probability of being sanctioned after cheating A. A will cooperate for each $b > 0$. Therefore, if the size of the sanction is very big, the

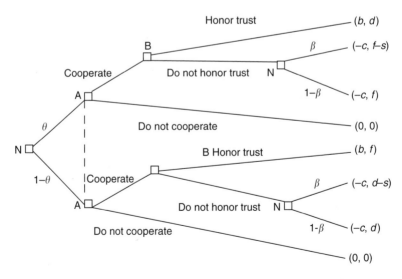

Figure 6.2   The game of social trust with a sanctioning State with incomplete information

probability of a sanction from the State may be low, and, even in that case, player B can honor trust. If selling poor-quality goods implies the death penalty, it is possible that the seller will avoid doing so, even if the probability of being sanctioned is very low. This conclusion is pitifully reactionary: the greater the sanction, the lower the necessity of efficacy in its application, because its dissuasive effects will be higher. Beccaria or Carrara would be probably shocked by this logic of criminal justice. Fortunately, the game depicted in figure 6.2 also has a more positive reading: the greater the efficacy of the State in applying sanctions, the lower these sanctions need be for player B not to cheat player A.

Games in figures 6.1 and 6.2 illustrate, therefore, how the State's sanctioning power facilitates the fulfillment of agreements. It fosters cooperation, but, does it foster trust? The answer is yes, it does. In the game in figure 6.2, which depicts the most realistic case in which the State does not have full information, player A updates his expectations about player B's trustworthiness in accordance with the sanctioning capacity of the State. If the sanctioning capacity of the State, that is, the probability of detecting and sanctioning the noncompliance of agreement β, is such that $\beta > (d - f)/s$, then both types of player B will be trustworthy. In this case, player A updates his beliefs about player B's trustworthiness, from θ (so that $0 \leq \theta \leq 1$) to 1. Thus, the presence of a State acting as a guarantor of agreements, does not just promote cooperation because it reduces the payoff to player B for cheating player A, but because it increases A's subjective expectations (i.e., his trust) with respect to player B's trustworthiness.

A second problem, noted by Goodin (2000) is the possible existence of a *trade-off* between State intervention through the courts, and voluntary fulfillment of agreements by individuals. That is, it may be the case that if the State is responsible for enforcing agreements, individuals will be less willing to fulfil them spontaneously. If State intervention does not compensate for the decrease in individual willingness to spontaneously fulfil agreements, the outcome could be greater noncompliance of agreements. In this case, we are dealing with the game shown in figure 6.3. In this game, the payoffs for the nonspontaneous compliance of agreements are reduced by amount φ. The outcome is that a trustworthy B will honor the trust placed in him if $\beta > (f - d + \varphi)/s$, while an opportunistic B will do the same when $\beta > (d - f + \varphi)/s$. The State, therefore, will have to apply tougher sanctions in order to assure fulfillment of agreements. However, I do not think that this objection should be taken too seriously. Goodin (2000) considers that the work of the courts may have a "crowding out effect" with respect to positive motives

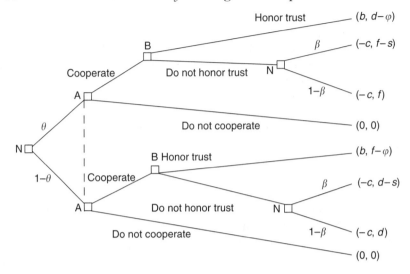

Figure 6.3   The game of social trust with a *trade-off* between spontaneous fulfillment of agreements and State intervention

to cooperate (in this case, to honor trust placed in an individual). This he calls a "demoralization effect." However, the idea that "if courts do their job, why fulfill an agreement?" is curious reasoning from someone who will be sanctioned if he does not comply. The presence of sanctioning courts could, in any case, reduce the truster's willingness to monitor agreements (i.e., it could make him more trusting). I think, therefore, that we should limit ourselves to the conclusions of the games in figures 6.1 and 6.2. Moreover, we could offer a more plausible reading of Goodin's objection. It could be the case that rather than undermining the individual's disposition to spontaneously fulfill agreements, the existence of sanctions reduces the disposition to trust the trustee. The presence of a sanction could favor the decision to fulfill the agreement, given the potential costs of noncompliance, but could also be a signal of distrust among parties to the agreement. However, we can easily overcome this objection, given that in this case the sanction is provided by a neutral third party (the State), and, therefore, is not necessarily a signal of distrust (Leibenstein, 1987).

The hypothesis derived from this section is, therefore, that the more effective the State as a guarantor of agreements, the more social trust will be developed. I now test this hypothesis. In order to do so, I have used data from 12 countries included in the 1990–91 wave of the World Value

Surveys. These countries are Argentina, Brazil, Denmark, Italy, Germany, Netherlands, Japan, South Korea, Spain, Sweden, United Kingdom, and United States. I include, therefore, both developed and less-developed countries. The levels of social trust in these countries (the percentage of respondents who think that "most people can be trusted" is shown in table 6.1). As can be seen, there are important differences in social trust between the Scandinavian countries, on the one hand, where 55–60 percent of people think that most people can be trusted, and countries such as Argentina, where this percentage is just 20 percent, and Brazil, where social trusters are just 6.4 percent. I test here the hypothesis that part of the explanation for these differences lies in the relative efficacy of the State as a guarantor of agreements.

To test this hypothesis, an indicator of the efficacy of the State as a guarantor of agreements is required. I have used, as a proxy, an index of individual perception of governmental corruption developed by the International Transparency Center for Corruption Research. I have used the 1995 index, compiled from seven surveys. Each of these surveys measures the subjective perception of corruption of office holders. Table 6.2 presents the results of the index for the 20 countries in my sample. The higher figures correspond to the lowest levels of corruption.

This table shows major national variations in perceptions of governmental corruption. At first sight, this might appear to be a good indicator of government's efficacy in sanctioning fraudulent breaches of agreements. It is to expected that in those countries in which office holders are less corrupt, they will apply legal norms more efficiently. One problem with this index is that it is not objective. It simply reflects

Table 6.1 Social trust, percentage that says that most people can be trusted

Sweden	59.6
Denmark	55.5
Netherlands	50.7
United States	49.5
United Kingdom	42.4
Japan	37.6
Italy	33.8
South Korea	33.6
Spain	32.1
Germany	31.1
Argentina	22.4
Brazil	6.4

Source: World Value Surveys, 1990.

Table 6.2   Citizen's perception of
the level of governmental corruption

Denmark	9.55
Sweden	8.87
Netherlands	8.69
United Kingdom	8.57
Germany	8.14
United States	7.79
Japan	6.72
Argentina	5.24
Spain	4.35
South Korea	4.29
Italy	2.99
Brazil	2.70

Source: Transparency International, 1995.

the perception of levels of corruption among the citizens of the country. However, this is not necessarily a fundamental problem. The application of sanctions by the State fosters social trust because individuals anticipate that fraudulent practices will be discouraged by State action. Citizens' belief in the State's capacity to effectively fulfill this role can be expected to be more or less well grounded. This is what the index reflects: citizens' perceptions of the degree of corruption among office holders. The hypothesis I am testing requires, as an index of the State's efficiency in applying sanctions, an index of citizens' perception of that efficiency, and this is the kind of information provided by the index in table 6.2.

In order to test the hypothesis I have developed a multilevel model, as this allows me to estimate simultaneously various levels in my data, and this improves estimation at both the individual and the aggregate level. In this case, the two levels of analysis are countries and individuals. Normally, one-level models analyze variations between countries at an aggregate level, identifying, for example, the extent to which countries with higher levels of public expenditure have higher levels of participation in associations. Other one-level studies analyze variations in participation among individuals, and examine the relevance of individual characteristics in influencing the probability of participation. Aggregate-level models have often been criticized because of the risks of ecological fallacies. Models that analyze differences between individuals do not face this problem, but sometimes they cannot test, or only indirectly, the effects of institutional variables on individual behavior (Jones and Bullen, 1994). My multilevel model, however, allows me to analyze both types of variation—between countries as well as between individuals. The dependent variable is social trust (value 0 = do not trust unknown people, value 1 = trust). Among the independent variables, I have included the corruption perception index. As control variables, I have used, on the one hand, some of the variables commonly associated with social trust in the social capital literature. More specifically, these are membership of associations and church attendance. The latter is not as far-fetched as it may sound, as numerous scholars of social capital, notably Putnam, attribute almost miraculous effects of religion and religious practice on social capital.[3] On the other hand, I have also used classic as control variable social class. I have distinguished four class strata: capitalists, petty bourgeoisie, new middle class, and working class. I have chosen these class categories drawing on the work of Erik Olin Wright (1997). As the variable for occupation used in the World Value Survey does not construct all of Wright's 12 positions in the class structure, the contradictory class positions that account for eight of Wright's 12 positions have all been grouped into a single category, the "new middle class."[4] As is the case in Wright's analysis, the distinction between capitalists and small employers is based on the number of employees (more or less than ten). The distinction between salaried workers who form a part of the "new middle class" and the traditional working class is based on differences in credentials and authority in the workplace, which means at the same time differences in exploitation and domination. In the multilevel model, the category of reference is, for the remaining classes, the capitalist class.

The results of the multilevel logistic model are shown in table 6.3. As I have said, multilevel models are designed to analyze variation across countries and across individuals. The parameter μ_{1j} captures the variation across countries. As it can be seen, the differences in trust across countries is significant. The variable introduced to explain these differences in the level of trust across countries is the efficiency of the State, measured through the corruption index. The results seem to confirm the hypothesis regarding the impact of State efficiency on the development of social trust. The variable "corruption" is significant and the sign of the coefficient is as predicted: the lower the perception of corruption among office holders, the higher the level of trust in unknown people. This can be more clearly seen in figure 6.4, which shows the predicted probabilities of trusting unknown people for different levels of perceived corruption. The predicted probabilities have been calculated allowing the variable for corruption to vary and setting the noncategorical variables in their means. The categorical variables—associational membership and

Table 6.3 Multilevel logit model, efficiency of the State and social trust (dependent var.: social trust)

Variables	Coefficients
Corruption	.170★★★
	(.058)
Gender	−.001
	(.001)
Size of town	−.006
	(.011)
Petty bourgeoisie	−.266
	(.153)
New middle class	.202★★★
	(.076)
Working class	−.336★★★
	(.075)
Education	−.001
	(.001)
Church attendance	−.025★★
	(.009)
Associational membership	.446★★★
	(.049)
μ_{1j}	.206★★★
	(.094)
Constant	−1.58★★★
	(.43)

Notes: Standard errors between brackets. ★★★ Significant at 99 percent. ★★ Significant at 95 percent. ★ Significant at 90 percent.

Source: *World Value Surveys*.

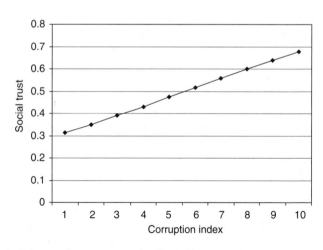

Figure 6.4 Influence of corruption among office holders on social trust

new middle class—take value one. As can be seen in figure 6.4, the lower the perception of corruption, the higher the social trust. In countries in which office holders have a reputation for honesty, the probability of trust (controlling by the set of variables in table 6.3) is 36 percent higher than in countries with high levels of corruption. For example, a new middle-class citizen who is a member of an association, who goes to church and lives in Brazil, has a probability of 31 percent to trust unknown people. By contrast, that same new middle-class citizen, living in Denmark has a probability of 67 percent to trust unknown people.

In terms of the control variables, church attendance is significant (challenging the traditional view of social capitalists), education, and one of the class categories, small employers. The other three class categories: capitalists, petty bourgeoisie, and new middle class, express less distrust in unknown people than the working class. Moreover, the higher the income, the lower the distrust. The main variable for social capitalist is also significant, but in the opposite direction to that expected: membership of associations is linked to lower levels of social trust.

This empirical test, based on a sample of 12 countries, supports the hypothesis that a State which acts as a guarantor of agreements fosters social trust. I now examine an indirect way in which the State can create social trust, namely by promoting membership of associations. This is indirect only if we accept the arguments of this chapter, that membership of associations generates social trust. In the next section, I analyze this new role of the State in the creation of social trust.

The State and Participation in Associations as an Indirect Way of Creating Social Trust

In the section dealing with external solutions to the collective-action dilemma, when discussing the overall role of the State in the creation of social capital, it was argued that the State could act as an external agent providing selective incentives to overcome collective-action dilemmas. This general framework of State action in the generation of social capital has been applied to the creation of social trust. The role of the State is rather more ambiguous in the case of participation in associations.

First, we need to consider the idea that associations are indeed a form of social capital. In my view, this is not the case. Social capital is a resource derived from participation in a given social network. This is part of the definition of social capital developed in chapter 2. Membership of a social network is a necessary condition of enjoyment of this kind of capital, and the kind of network largely determines the type of social capital you obtain from it. Participation in associations may produce social capital in terms of private information, relations of trust between the members of the association (and the obligations of reciprocity attached to such relations of trust), and, possibly, social trust. Therefore, if the State plays a positive role in creating voluntary associations, it also contributes indirectly to the generation of social capital.

As we have seen, the studies of social capital more often attribute a negative rather than a positive role to the State with respect to associations. As noted earlier, according to these authors, the rise of the modern State destroyed the social capital that existed in *ancien régime* societies. Perhaps we should regret the destruction, for example, of those guilds in which the apprentices were generally ill-treated, or those idyllic peasant communities plagued, according to Popkin, by distrust and selfishness. Similarly, it is argued that the Soviet State set out to destroy social capital. Certain actions of modern democratic States, such as the 1960s urban development policies implemented in the United States, have also been criticized for destroying local communities and social capital (Putnam, 1993b, 2000).

I have already noted that this distrust of State action with regard to voluntary associations is related to largely conservative arguments, intended to defend civil society against the State.[5] However, we can also find distrust of the State in some contemporary analyses of participative democracy. For example, in Paul Hirst's conception of associative democracy (1994). According to Hirst, one condition for the growth of associations is a reduction in the size of the State.[6]

In contrast to these authors, I argue that the State can promote participation in associations in various ways. It is useful here to distinguish between direct and indirect State action in favor of participation in associations.

The most obvious of the different types of action directly intended to favor associationism is the concession of financial support. The State can promote voluntary associations by giving them grants, tax breaks, or access to and use of public premises. Through such policies, the State can have a significant impact on the costs of participation in associations. These minor costs are especially important in the case of private-good associations, but they are also of some importance for public-good associations. In a private-good association, for example, a choral society, the specific good (in this case, singing beautiful songs with other talented people) can only be achieved by participating in the association.

Nevertheless, the creation of the association can be made much easier by public support, for example, because members of the association do not have the necessary resources to maintain it alone. In the case of public-good associations, we are faced with a collective-action problem. If this collective-action problem is a prisoner's dilemma, the outcome is that nobody will contribute to the public good. As we have seen, a possible solution to this type of collective-action problem is a sanction applied by the State. The State sanction can be positive or negative. The subsidy would act as a positive incentive for participation. For example, during the New Deal, many associations received subsidies from the U.S. government. Some of these associations, such as the American Farm Bureau Federation received grants from the Agriculture Department and were clearly public-good associations (Skocpol, 1997). In general, State subsidies are the most important source of funds for voluntary associations (Nowland-Foreman, 1998: 113). These subsidies can serve, for example, to reduce the monetary contribution that each member must make to the association. The influence of minor costs on the decision to participate in a voluntary association is, in any event, limited. The free-rider problem is mainly associated with the impossibility of excluding from the public good those who have not participated in its provision. For example, agrarian reform laws secured by the American Farm Bureau Federation benefited all American farmers, and not just the members of the Federation. The decision to participate does not depend, therefore, on the costs of participation. Even if those costs are very low, the problem of free-riding remains. If subsidies are given to individuals who participate in associations, subsidies may act as selective incentives to guarantee participation. Take the following historical example of the way selective incentives promote participation. In Athens in the fourth century B.C., citizens who participated in the *ekklesia*, or assembly of the people, were paid some money (Hansen, 1999: 150). The laws approved in the assembly were a public good, affecting all Athenian citizens, participants and nonparticipants alike. The one or one-and-a-half *drakmas* given to the first 6,000 participants in the assembly were a selective incentive for participation. With few exceptions,[7] however, modern States give subsidies to associations, rather than to individual members. Nevertheless, it may be the case that State subsidies provide sufficient resources to allow the association to offer selective incentives for participation. However, this possibility aside, the reduction of the costs of participation does not alter the collective-action problem in public-good associations.

Another way in which the State directly favors participation is through the institutionalization of certain types of associations. The development of Welfare States in western Europe after the Second World War was accompanied by the institutionalization of corporatist agreements between the government and the labor and employer organizations. This probably contributed to the expansion of the memberships of these organizations. Besides, Welfare States favored the development and expansion of other interest groups. According to Paul Pierson (1996), the major social programs developed by the Welfare State in fields of pensions, unemployment, education, and health care, benefited approximately half the electorate in developed countries. These public polices have created around them an extensive network of interest groups, such as for example, the American Association of Pensioners, with 28 million members. In this case, State pension policies created the interest around which the American Association of Pensioners developed. The social policies of the government created beneficiaries, and therefore, an interest in the expansion of these policies. The State provides reasons for participation in associations. Nevertheless, it has to be acknowledged that this State function is not of great significance. Even though the actions of the State can create interests in associations, if the aim of the association is a public good, there is still a temptation to be a free-rider.

Finally, the Welfare State can promote participation in associations indirectly, through its impact on individual variables. Numerous empirical studies have shown that certain individual characteristics are positively related to participation in voluntary associations. The most important of these characteristics are education and income (Verba et al., 1978, 1995: 27–33, 334–351; Rosentone and Hansen, 1993). Improvements in education and income provide the individual with resources that facilitate participation. A well-educated individual is a more competent participant. Her cognitive capacities lower the cost of participation in a voluntary association. There is also a relation between income and participation in associations, as the costs of participation usually include contributions to the funds of the association. Obviously, individuals with more economic resources will be better able to accept and meet those costs.

Individual resources, economic as well as educative, therefore, have a positive impact on participation in voluntary associations. The role of the State in this case is clear. The provision of education and the redistribution of income are two of the main features of modern Welfare States. Countries with more generous Welfare States are also those in which the distribution of income is more egalitarian and where educational levels are higher. Above certain minimum levels of welfare that allow individuals to participate, a more egalitarian distribution of income fosters higher participation in associations by the less well-off.

To sum up, directly or indirectly the State fosters participation in voluntary associations. This is clear in the case of private-good associations. The State grants subsidies to help set up associations. The Welfare State social policies distribute resources (financial and cognitive) to individuals that enable them to participate in associations, and social policies (education, pensions, health) create interests around which people organize. All these factors are also applicable in the case of public-good associations, although their impact is weaker. Any decrease in the costs of participation does not have a major impact on the incentives to behave as a free-rider. All we can say is that the resources provided to those associations by the State enable them to offer selective incentives for participation.[8]

Hence, the hypothesis derived from this last section is that the greater the size of the Welfare State, the greater the probability of participation in associations (and, thus, the greater the creation of social capital).

In order to test this hypothesis I have used data on 12 countries from the 1990–91 wave of the World Value Survey (see table 6.4). The previous sample of 12 countries has been slightly modified to include just developed countries: Austria, Canada, Denmark, Germany, Netherlands, Italy, Japan, Norway, Spain, Sweden, United Kingdom, and United States. This is because these countries produce much more reliable public expenditure figures. These countries display strong differences in terms

Table 6.4 Membership of at least one association (in percent)

Sweden	83.5
Netherlands	82.7
Norway	78.9
Denmark	78.9
United States	70.6
Germany	63.9
Canada	61.6
Austria	49.7
United Kingdom	49.7
Italy	32.6
Japan	30.7
Spain	22

Source: World Value Surveys, 1990.

of the dependent variable (participation in associations). These differences are shown in table 6.4.

Table 6.5 shows the levels of public expenditure as a percentage of GDP for the 12 countries in 1990. In order to test the hypothesis—the influence of the State on participation in voluntary associations—I have developed a multilevel model, given that, as I have already said this allows me to estimate simultaneously various levels in my data, and this improves estimation at both the individual and the aggregate level. In this case, the two levels of analysis are also countries and individuals.

In this model, the dependent variable is membership in voluntary associations (value 0 = non members, value 1 = members of at least one association). As a dichotomous dependent variable, we assume a binomial distribution in the model. The independent variables are levels of public expenditure as a percentage of GDP, used here as a proxy for the size of the Welfare State in each country and six control variables. These are educational level, population of place of residence,[9] social class in four categories—capitalist class, petty bourgeoisie, new middle class, and working class (with the capitalist class as category of reference)—and level of social trust as a dichotomous variable with value 1 for trust in unknown people and value 2 for distrust (with value 1 as the category of reference).

The results of the multilevel model are shown in table 6.6. The results in table 6.6 show that the public expenditure variable is significant. This means that the higher the level of public expenditure, the greater the

Table 6.5 Public expenditure as a percentage of GDP (1990)

Sweden	59.1
Denmark	57.6
Netherlands	56.8
Austria	56.4
Italy	53.2
Norway	49.7
Canada	46.7
Germany	45.9
Spain	42.1
United Kingdom	39.1
United States	33.6
Japan	31.3

Source: Commission of the European Union, OECD, World Bank Development Indicators (1999).

Table 6.6 Multilevel logit model, the State and participation in associations

Variables	Coefficients
Public expenditure	.082★★★
	(.023)
Working class	−.016
	(.083)
Petty bourgeoisie	.147
	(.154)
New middle class	.115
	(.084)
Social trust	−.372★★★
	(.050)
Education	.124★★★
	(.010)
Size of town	−.019 ★
	(.011)
μ_{1j}	.557★★★
	(.232)
Constant	−3.495★★★
	(1.054)

Notes: Standard errors in brackets. ★★★ Significant at 99 percent. ★ Significant at 90 percent.

Source: *World Value Surveys*.

probability of joining an association, a result in line with the hypothesis tested. This can be seen clearly in figure 6.5, which shows the probabilities of joining an association for a member of the new middle class. In this figure, all the other variables in the model have been kept constant at their averages. The probability of an average individual, a member of the new middle class, with an average level of education and income, joining an association in a country with public expenditure of 30 percent of GDP, as Japan, is 46 percent, while the probability of joining an association for this same new middle class individual is 60 percent in a country with public expenditure of 60 percent of GDP, like for example, Sweden.

Among the control variables, educational level is significant (the higher the educational level, the higher the probability of joining an association) and social trust (lower levels of social trust are linked to a lesser probability of joining an association). The "Putnamite" variable introduced in the model—the size of the town—is practically insignificant.

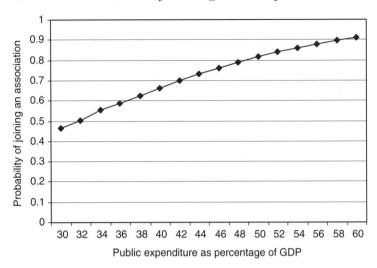

Figure 6.5   The size of the State and the probability of joining an association

Moreover, the direction of the coefficient is not that predicted by the literature: the larger the town, the lower the probability of joining an association.

Another conclusion that can be drawn from this model is that variables of social class are not significant. This is a rather surprising result, which may be explained by the inability of the aggregate analysis to capture some of the differences in participation in associations between social classes. Apart from the level of expenditure, the type of Welfare State could be expected to have an influence on the levels of participation. For example, social democratic Welfare States, such as Sweden, Denmark, Norway, or Austria (which are more egalitarian according to Esping-Andersen (1993)) could be expected to provide more favorable conditions for working-class participation, than Liberal or Conservative Welfare States.

In order to test this hypothesis, it is worth taking a look at the percentages of participation in associations by social class. These are shown in table 6.7. We can see, on the one hand, that in most cases (nine out of 12), participation is lower among the working class. On the other hand, in the social democratic Welfare States, we see that the index of participation is very high for the working class (83.5 percent in Sweden, 71.1 percent in Norway, 74.1 percent in Denmark). In Sweden,

Table 6.7   Percentage of members of at least one association by social class

	Capitalists	Small employers	Petty bourgeoisie	New middle class	Working class
Sweden	72.5	75.8	82.4	84.4	83.5
Netherlands	100	78.8	88.2	87.7	70.5
Norway	84.7	73.8	72.7	85	71.1
United States	72.9	78.1	73.9	74.4	58.7
Germany	87.5	59.2	67.3	66.5	51.9
Canada	65.3	63.1	68.4	68.4	54.5
United Kingdom	58.6	60.7	61.5	57.5	34.1
Japan	35.6	37.5	34.5	32	32.1
Spain	40	21.8	17.1	29.7	18.2
Denmark	80	63.2	70.4	83.3	74.1
Austria	49.5	—	39.8	57.3	39
Italy	52.4	34.4	22.5	41.4	22.3

Source: *World Value Surveys*, 1990.

the levels of participation of the working class are even higher than those of the other classes except the new middle class.

Nevertheless, table 6.7 shows differences that may not be significant once we have controlled for other variables in a more complex statistical analysis. I consider this possibility in the remainder of this section. First, I test to see whether the scale of the Welfare State (but not the type of Welfare State) affects levels of participation in associations by social class. That is, whether higher levels of public expenditure have a greater impact on levels of participation for some social classes than for others, or whether the effect is uniformly distributed across social classes. In order to examine this issue, I have run a multilevel model in which the dependent variable is, as in the model of table 6.6, participation in associations. Along with the independent variables of the model presented in table 6.7, I have now added interactions between expenditure and the three categories of class: interaction between public expenditure and the new middle class, between public expenditure and petty bourgeoisie, and between public expenditure and working class.[10] The category of reference is the capitalist class. The results of this model are shown in table 6.8. It can be seen that public expenditure remains significant and that the direction of the coefficient is the same as in the previous model: the higher the level of public expenditure, the greater the probability of participation in associations. In terms of the control variables, trust is significant (the greater the distrust of unknown people, the lower

Table 6.8   Multilevel logit model, the State and participation in associations with interactions between public expenditure and social class

Variables	Coefficients
Public expenditure	.063★★★
	(.024)
Working class	− 1.155★★★
	(.438)
Petty bourgeoisie	−.139
	(.681)
New middle class	−.699
	(.425)
Interaction: public expenditure-working class	.027★★★
	(.010)
Interaction: public expenditure-petty bourgeoisie	.007
	(.016)
Interaction: public expenditure-new middle class	.020★★
	(.010)
Social trust	−.368★★★
	(.050)
Education	.124 ★★★
	(.010)
Size of town	−.020★
	(.011)
μ_{1j}	.563★★★
	(.255)
Constant	−2.695★★★
	(1.115)

Notes: Standard errors in brackets. ★★★ Significant at 99 percent. ★★ Significant at 95 percent. ★ Significant at 90 percent.

Source: *World Value Surveys.*

the probability of joining an association) and education (the more educated the person, the greater the probability of joining an association). The size of place of residence is significant in this case, and confirms in this case the "Putnamite" insight: the probability of joining an association is lower in larger cities.

What about social class? Taking the capitalist class as the category of reference, the probability of joining associations if the individual is a member of the working class is significantly lower than if he is a member of the capitalist class. That is, while the Welfare State may imply higher levels of participation, this is concentrated among the privileged (or exploitative, in Wright's analysis[11]) social classes. The most interesting result of this model, however, concerns the interaction terms.

These interaction terms reflect the variation in the probability of join-ing an association for members of the new middle class, the petty bour-geoisie, or the working class, all in comparison to the capitalist class, for increasing levels of public expenditure. In the case of the new middle class and the working class, the interaction is significant. This implies that an increase in public expenditure does not affect all social classes equally in terms of the probability of them joining an association. An increase in levels of public expenditure has a stronger positive impact on the prob-ability of members of the working class joining an association than is the case of members of the capitalist class. Thus, as we expected, an increase in public expenditure is not only associated with higher levels of partic-ipation in general, but also with a more egalitarian distribution of the probability of joining an association. This is clearly shown in figure 6.6, that shows the predicted probabilities of joining an association for the members of the two social classes—the capitalist class and the working class—for different levels of public expenditure. In countries with lower levels of public expenditure (Japan, with 31 percent), there is a difference of 27 percentage points in the probability of joining an association between the two social classes. This difference drops to just 19 percent-age points in the countries with the highest levels of public expenditure.

This analysis shows how the size of the State influences the distri-bution of the probability of joining an association among different

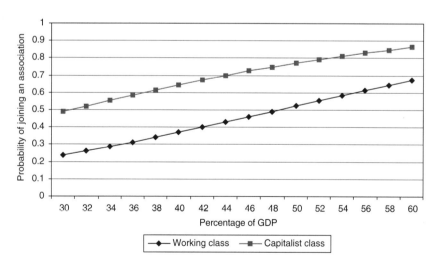

Figure 6.6   The size of the state and the probability of joining an association for different social classes

social classes. To end this section, I now test whether this distribution among social classes is also influenced by the type of Welfare State. I have considered, along with Esping-Andersen's work (1993) three types of Welfare State: the social democratic one, the Conservative one, and the Liberal one. In order to do so, I have estimated three logistic regressions using three countries from my sample: Sweden, with a social democratic Welfare State, the United States, with a Liberal one, and Spain, with a Welfare State that resembles a Conservative model.

The first model, for Sweden, is shown in table 6.9. The dependent variable is participation in associations. The independent variables are the same as in the general model shown in table 6.8. I have added a "Putnamite" variable: church attendance, just to test incidentally the hypothesis about the positive impact of church attendance in the

Table 6.9 Sweden, logit regression, dependent variable: participation in associations

Variables	Coefficients
Social trust	.193
	(.207)
Capitalists	−.899★
	(.541)
Small employers	−.646
	(.597)
Petty bourgeoisie	−.252
	(.556)
New middle class	.085
	(.370)
Political interest	−.410★★★
	(.132)
Church attendance	−.095
	(.069)
Size of town	−.113★★
	(.052)
Age	.000
	(.001)
Education	.123★★★
	(.053)
Gender	.279
	(.203)
Constant	4.136★★★
	(.807)

Notes: Standard errors in brackets. ★★★ Significant at 99 percent.
★★ Significant at 95 percent. ★ Significant at 90 percent.

Source: World Value Surveys.

probability of joining an association. This is a continuous variable with a range from 1 to 8, where 1 means attend religious services more than once a week, and 8, is for those who never attend religious services. The category of reference for social classes is the working class. We can see that one of the social class variables, the capitalist class, is significant. The sign of the coefficient indicates that the members of the capitalist class have a lower probability of joining an association than members of the working class.

This result can more clearly be seen in figure 6.7. In Sweden, the probability of joining an association for members of the working class is 16 percent higher than for members of the capitalist class. As for the control variables, political interest is significant (people who are more interested in politics are more likely to join an association), and one of the three "social capital" variables: the smaller the town, the higher the probability of joining an association. We find no evidence of the "miraculous" effects of church attendance (although the coefficient is in the expected direction, it is insignificant, and nor is social trust linked to participation in associations in this case. The effects of the levels of education on the probability of participation in associations are the expected ones: the higher the educational level, the higher the probability of joining an association.

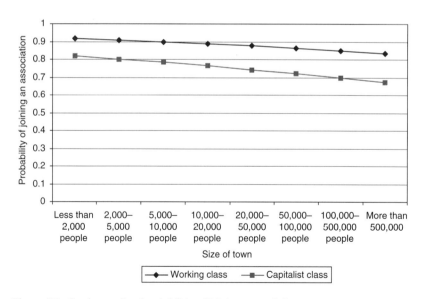

Figure 6.7 Sweden, predicted probabilities of joining an association

The results are very different for the United States, where levels of participation are relatively high. In spite of the so-called decline of civic America the United States ranks sixth in the sample in terms of participation in associations. Thus, it seems that the United States has not completely lost its skill in the associative art that so impressed Tocqueville. Furthermore, participation is very high in spite of its small Welfare State. However, behind the aggregate figures lie strong differences between social classes. These differences appear clearly in table 6.10, which shows the result of the logit model of participation in associations for the United States. Controlling for the most common variables, we can see that two class categories show significant differences in participation in associations. As in the previous model, the category of reference for

Table 6.10 United States, logit regression, dependent variable: participation in associations

Variables	Coefficients
Social trust	.236*
	(.140)
Capitalists	.542
	(.354)
Small employers	.706**
	(.318)
Petty bourgeoisie	−.060
	(.568)
New middle class	.586***
	(.171)
Political interest	−.294***
	(.080)
Age	.000
	(.001)
Gender	.223
	(.140)
Education	.123***
	(.045)
Church attendance	−.319***
	(.034)
Size of town	−.036
	(.032)
Constant	2.924***
	(.431)

Notes: Standard errors in brackets. *** Significant at 99 percent. ** Significant at 95 percent. * Significant at 90 percent.

Source: *World Value Surveys*, 1990.

social classes is the working class. Both the small employers and the members of the new middle class have a higher probability of joining an association than members of the working class. This is the opposite result to that found in Sweden. This result is more clearly shown in figure 6.8.

Figure 6.8 shows that the probability of joining an association in the United States is 10 percent higher if you are a member of the capitalist class than if you are a member of the working class, irrespective of the size of the town where you live. With respect to the control variables, political interest is significant (the stronger the political interest, the greater the probability of joining an association), and also social trust (social trusters are more likely to join associations), church attendance (church attendance increases significantly in the United States the probability of joining an association), and education (that has a positive impact, as expected, in the probability of joining an association).

This same "U.S." result is found in the Spanish case. In Spain the aggregate levels of participation in associations are very low, but, as in the other countries, social classes behave differently in this respect. Table 6.11 depicts the logistic model for Spain. As we can see, capitalists and members of the new middle class tend to join associations more than the working class, once we have controlled for the same variables as in the other two models. These differences are clearly visible in figure 6.9.

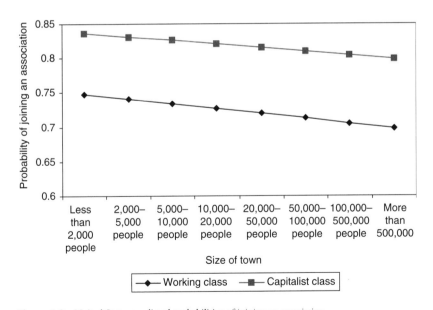

Figure 6.8 United States, predicted probabilities of joining an association

Table 6.11 Spain, logistic regression, dependent
variable: participation in associations

Variables	Coefficients
Social Trust	.336**
	(.114)
Capitalists	.829*
	(.457)
Small employers	.249
	(.201)
Petty bourgeoisie	.319
	(.388)
New middle class	.514***
	(.131)
Political interest	−.347***
	(.059)
Age	−.008**
	(.004)
Gender	.224*
	(.122)
Education	.123***
	(.050)
Church attendance	−.051*
	(.030)
Size of town	.074**
	(.027)
Constant	−.238
	(.385)

Notes: Standard errors in brackets. *** Significant at
99 percent. ** Significant at 95 percent. * Significant
at 90 percent.

Source: World Value Surveys, 1990.

Members of the capitalist class have a 10–16 percent higher probability
(depending on the size of their town) of joining an association than
members of the working class. As for the control variables, all of them
are significant, including those which attract most attention from social
capitalists: church attendance (the less frequent the attendance to religious services, the lower the probability of joining an association), size of
town (although in the opposite direction to that expected: the probability of joining an association is higher the greater the size of the town)
and social trust (social trusters tend to associate with each other).
Education is also significant, and has a positive effect on the probability
of joining an association, as in the previous models.

We can conclude, therefore, that the State plays an indirect role in
creating social trust through its influence on participation in associations.

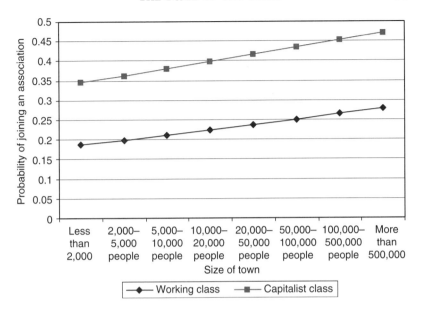

Figure 6.9 Spain, predicted probabilities of joining an association

People tend to participate more in associations in countries with larger Welfare States. Furthermore, higher public expenditure is associated with greater equality in the distribution of social capital. Social capitalists should bear in mind that decisive intervention by the State in the creation of social capital can lead not just to bigger stocks of this resource, but to greater equality in its distribution.

Conclusions

What can we conclude from the previous sections, and from the findings about social trust in chapter 5? We now have new clues as to the answer to one of the questions posed at the beginning of this book: why are some communities blessed with larger stocks of social capital than others? We know that social and particularized trust can be created as by-products of participation in associations. And we also know that the State can promote participation in associations, and that, in a context of uncertain and costly information about the other's preferences, signs can be used strategically to create trust. In these mechanisms lie, to a large extent, the explanation for the differences in social capital between communities. This is something that I explore in chapter 7.

CHAPTER SEVEN

The "Virtuous Circle" of the Creation of Social Capital

I began this book with a question: how can we explain differences between communities in terms of their stock of social capital? My contention has been that the creation of social capital as a by-product of other activities, including participation in associations, is only part of the answer. We have, nonetheless, come some way toward accounting for that difference. In this chapter I incorporate some of the previous arguments, and add new ones, to present a model of a "virtuous circle" generating social capital.

We have explored different ways of creating particularized and social trust. Some of these are more helpful than others in explaining the differences in social capital between communities. The role of the State is especially promising in this sense. The answer as to why varying levels of social capital exist between countries, may lie in the different roles played by State in promoting participation in associations, for example, or in their efficacy in the enforcement of agreements. However, even if the ways of creating social capital examined in the previous chapters were sufficient to explain the initial variations between different communities, this may be insufficient to explain why those differences survive through time. In acknowledging this, I seem to implicitly be giving weight to Putnam's belief that social capital survived in the center and north of Italy for ten centuries. Actually, it is not necessary to go so far. The idea that an initial impetus in the creation of social capital was maintained throughout this period because that impetus created a "virtuous circle" lacks credibility. More still in the light of events in Italy those ten centuries that would appear sufficiently powerful to have destroyed the existing stocks of social capital. This should be read merely as a warning not to overestimate the capacity of social capital to create more social capital.

In this chapter, I defend the idea that social capital can generate more social capital. I present a model of a virtuous circle in the creation of social capital.

The virtuous circle begins with the creation of trust relations as a by-product of participation in associations (although, in fact, social capital can be created as a by-product of participation in any type of social network, formal or informal, such as, e.g., friendship relations). The decision to participate in an association may be motivated by different considerations, one of which is State provision of selective incentives to participate. Trust relations created by participation in associations can constitute either social or particularized trust. Now, we reach the key element in the virtuous circle: those relations of trust foster the creation of, and participation in new associations. This is how social capital creates more social capital. Trust may be important for the creation of private-good associations, but its main importance lies in its role in the creation of public-good associations.

Why may social trust be important for the creation of public-good associations? The constitution of this last type of association involves a social dilemma. One of the solutions to this dilemma may lie in the existence of relations of particularized trust, or, above all, social trust. I address this issue more fully later.

Figure 7.1 presents an outline of the model of the virtuous circle of social capital. The story of the virtuous circle depicted in this figure is rather like the "story of two cities." In one of them, the State provides subsidies to constitute new associations and has an efficient public administration. This is made more likely by the fact that citizens, thanks to their higher stocks of social capital, can make their local government more accountable. State support makes associations more common. As a consequence of all this, citizens learn to trust unknown people, and build strong relations of particularized trust with members of their associations. These relations of trust facilitate the association of citizens with a common interest, because each knows that his trust will be honored.

On the other hand, in the other city the government does not promote the development of associations. Moreover, inefficiency and corruption in the administration (fostered, among other things, by the lack of social capital, which hinders citizens' capacity to organize and demand their rights) make contracting risky. Citizens incur high transaction costs in monitoring of agreements, because there is no State to rely on. As a

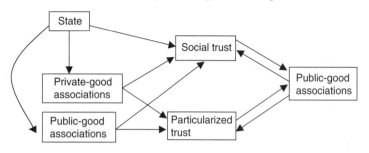

Figure 7.1   The virtuous circle in the creation of social capital

result, most citizens think that it is not worth trusting unknown people. Social distrust is, at the same time, an obstacle to the development of associations.

The story of the two cities illustrates in a rather naive way the two ideal processes of virtuous and vicious circles of social capital. In order to offer a rather less simplistic illustration of these same processes, I draw on two historical examples of the virtuous circle in action. The first involves the story of two Italian towns and the second, English craftsmen at the end of the eighteenth century.

My first example involves the two Italian towns of Trasacco and Luco dei Marsi. Both towns are located in the Fucino basin in the Abruzzo region in central Italy. They are both largely agricultural towns that were affected by the agrarian reforms that led to the expropriation of most of the large estates and the redistribution of the land to the landless peasants and small tenant farmers. Both towns have been exposed to similar pressures and influences throughout their history but, nonetheless, showed remarkable differences in terms of their political activities, relations of friendship and values.[1] Trasacco was plagued by low levels of participation in associations, types of friendship dominated by clientelism, and negative attitudes toward interpersonal trust. Conversely, Luco shows high levels of participation, the virtual nonexistence of clientelist networks, egalitarian values, positive attitudes toward interpersonal trust, and high levels of political involvement.

Luco and Trasacco could be portrayed as parallel stories of the success and failure of the organization for collective action. Luco has a remarkable tradition of social struggle that perhaps began with the conflict of various groups of *luchesi* against the drainage of the lake in which they fished. The drainage was finally carried out in the mid-nineteenth century by order of the Prince of Torlonia, who counted on the backing of the newly formed Italian State. At the end of the nineteenth- and the beginning of the twentieth century, and above all during *Bienio Rosso* (1919–21), the Socialist and Communist movements were far stronger in Luco than in any other area of the Fucino basin. So too was the opposition against fascism before and after 1922. After the war, the expropriation of the Prince of Torlonia's lands was led by members of the *Partito Comunista Italiano* (PCI), and the protagonists were mainly *luchesi* who had taken part in the *Lotta dei Fucino*. Conversely, in Trasacco there was no opposition to the usurpation of the fishing rights in the lake by the Roman Colonna family in the Middle Ages, nor to the drainage of the lake in the nineteenth century. During the first two decades of the twentieth century, while Socialist and Communist organizations were quickly developing in Luco, they scarcely made any inroads in Trasacco. They only had any success in the two or three years following the First World War. In the previous period up to the expropriation of the Torlonia estates, during the *Lotta dei Fucino*, hardly any of the *trasaccani* supported the Communist Party that led the people of the Fucino basin. Most of the few Trasacco peasants who did support the PCI left the party after lands had been expropriated. After the war, politics in Trasacco was almost completely dominated by the Christian Democrats.

One important difference between the people of Luco and Trasacco is the type of relationships that exist within their own communities. Horizontal relations dominated Luco, while vertical ones characterized Trasacco. Although part of the literature treats all types of relations as sources of social capital, in chapter four I argued that vertical networks have a weaker capacity for the creation of relations of trust.

In Trasacco in 1865, before the drainage of the lake, 9.6 percent of the families (28 out of 290) had properties of over 5 hectares. In fact, two-thirds of the land in Trasacco (including church property) was controlled by 10 percent of the population. The other 90.4 percent had properties of under 1 hectare (that is, less than that considered necessary to maintain a family) or no land at all. These families were forced to rent land or work for the richer landowners. In general terms peasants depended on the large landowners for their survival. In Luco the situation was different. The distribution of land was far more equal. The largest landowners only controlled 9 percent of the land. The rest was distributed in a remarkably egalitarian way among 580 families, which each owned plots of over one hectare. There were no landless peasants. In terms of the predominance of these small farms and the absence of a small landowning elite, Luco had a far more economically homogenous population that Trasacco.

One outcome of the differences in the distribution of the land between Trasacco and Luco was that it favored the development of vertical relations of dependence in Trasacco, given that most of the peasants had to work the estates of the large landowners. It seems that clientelistic relations were widespread in Trasacco. An index of the presence of these types of relations commonly used is the number of votes won by individual candidates in elections, that is, the importance of "preference voting." In Italian elections, voters have the opportunity to assign individual votes to a limited number of candidates. Given that a clientelist politician asks his subordinates to vote first for him and second for the party, preference voting is a good index of clientelism in Italy. In the 1975 local elections, for example, there were 7,129 of these votes in Trasacco, an average of two for every voter, while this figure was just 217 out of an electorate of 3.041 in Luco.

One example of the predominance of vertical relations in Trasacco can be found in associational practices. Voluntary associations, such as the local football club, were dominated by a small group of Trasacco residents, the larger landowners. The development of relations of trust between superiors and subordinates in these kinds of associations was inhibited. According to Caroline White, relations between superiors and subordinates were fraught with "cynicism and suspicion." Nevertheless, there could still be relations of trust between landless peasants and small peasants. However, the development of relations of trust between poor peasants faced various obstacles, competition for scarce employment, for example, on the landowners' properties. This competition was a huge barrier to collective action. Another difficulty was the activities of the landowners against peasants' effort to organize for collective action. In spite of these obstacles, relations of trust did exist among peasants in Trasacco that were the source of social capital. For example, an institution called *comparaggio* meant a lifetime's relationship between the parents of a baptized child and the child's godparents. The aim of this was to establish obligations of reciprocity between parents and godparents. According to White, this link was culturally defined as an obligation. This meant that members of this relation had internalized a social norm that forced them to respect the relation of *comparaggio* and that noncompliance was sanctioned by some sort of internal sanction, such as shame.

In Luco there were fewer obstacles to the development of relations of trust. The distribution of property was much more egalitarian and peasants had the necessary means for their subsistence, so they were not dependent on the large landowners. Caroline White points to the existence of strong relations of trust among the *luchesi*. One especially important factor was the absence of relations of subordination, and, as a result, of obstacles to the development of relations of trust.

The distribution of property in both towns, therefore, favored the development of different types of social relations. In Luco, horizontal relations favored the development of systems of trust. In Trasacco, vertical relations were, to some extent, an obstacle to that development. A good example of the way in which this original difference affected the structure of associations in Luco and Trasacco is the management of various types of communal goods in both towns from the Middle Ages onward.

Another distinctive feature of Luco dei Marsi's inhabitants in comparison to those of Trasacco was that the former had had the right to fish in the lake from the Middle Ages, whereas the latter did not. In both communities, the Church formally controlled these rights, but in reality the people of both towns exercised them in exchange for a rent. In Trasacco, the Colonna family usurped these rights, whereas in Luco the people retained their rights. In the 1823 occupational census of the Fucino basin, 1,349 *luchesi* (33.5 percent of the total population) identified themselves as fishermen. This meant that fishing was their main activity. Nonetheless, the other 490 *luchesi*, classified as peasants in the census, also occasionally fished in the lake.

Fishermen used communally owned boats to fish in the lake. Groups of fishermen organized cooperatively to pay for the boat, fish together, and sell their produce in the regional market. The situation faced by the *luchesi* was a dilemma of the commons. Fishing was a common resource, and one that was important enough to make it costly (although not impossible) to exclude potential beneficiaries from profiting from it. Fishing was not a public good because the consumption of one unit of the resource (say, a ton of fish) reduced the quantity available to the others (Ostrom, 1990: 30–31; Ostrom et al., 1994: 6–7). We do not know exactly how the *luchesi* overcame their dilemma of the commons, although it seems that they did manage to do so, since the resource survived and supported most of Luco's population from the Middle Ages to the drainage of the lake in 1864–76. What we do know is that part of the institutional arrangement for the exploitation of the common resource included the use of collectively owned boats. Boats were built and manned by groups of *luchesi*. Luco fishermen worked together because they could not individually afford the costs of building and maintaining the boats. In this case they were not faced with a social dilemma. The boat was a private good, and all the people interested in fishing would form groups to build and maintain them.

There were also common-pool resources in Trasacco. Although *trasaccani* had lost their fishing rights to the lake, about 60 percent of Trasacco's total area consisted of communal land. This land was reserved for public use: all inhabitants had the right to use the land for pasture and as a source of wood. The local administration, the *università*, controlled access to these common-pool resources. In many peasant communities, the *università* included all members of the community (or those members that had the status of "free men," most of the population from the tenth century onward), who met together in an assembly (Reynolds, 1997: 110–113; Genicot, 1993). However, in Trasacco the local government was elected by a very small group of landowners and educated people. In 1865, this "electoral corps" included just 3 percent of the population. The *università*'s organizational structure gives us some clues about the way in which Trasacco managed its dilemma of the commons. To a certain extent, Trasacco's community was a privileged group in Mancur Olson's sense, given that a subgroup of its inhabitants, the large landowners, had an interest in organizing access to the common-pool resource (Olson, 1973: 49–50). It was relatively easy to monitor compliance with the rules governing use of the common resource. Given that the extraction of units from the resource depended on compliance with the governing rules by all users, each agent had an interest in monitoring the compliance of the others. Once an infraction of the rules was detected, the problem arose as to who would apply the sanction. This sanction was a public good in itself but the Trasacco community was, probably, a privileged group in this sense too, given that the subgroup of large landowners were responsible for imposing the sanctions. Large landowners had an interest in providing regulatory institutions and sanctions for access and maintenance of the common-pool resource, because the benefits they obtained were disproportionately large. They had far greater rights over the common resource, and control of the regulatory institutions confirmed the peasant's position of dependency. This is an example of how joint and unanimous strategies of conditional cooperation were unnecessary to overcome the dilemma of collective action. If there is a subgroup of agents with preferences of an assurance game that is able to coordinate in a cooperative equilibrium, the dilemma can be overcome. In Trasacco, those were the preferences of the landowners: they were all interested in creating regulatory rules for the communal lands, but none of them could provide those rules individually. However, the fact that this social dilemma was overcome does not imply more social capital derived from relations of trust, because the type of organization put into effect to overcome the dilemma was a vertical, nondemocratic one.

The histories of Luco and Trasacco illustrate some of the processes behind the generation of a virtuous circle of social capital creation. The origin of the differences in social capital derived from the relations of trust existing in the two towns lies in the management of the common-pool resources. In Luco, informal groups of fishermen joined together to share the costs of building a boat, and afterward worked communally to fish. In Trasacco, common-pool resources were managed by a subgroup of landowners that provided appropriate sanctions to maintain the common resource. The first type of arrangement is more prone than the second to the development of relations of trust, given its horizontal features (Trasacco's *università* was a vertical organization). This initial difference in the development of trust initiated a dynamic of social capital creation in Luco. Trust facilitated the development of public-good organizations for collective action, both when fishing rights were under threat and later, during the struggle for the partition of the land. At the same time, this fostered the development of new relations of trust. In Trasacco we do not find the same process: distrust inhibits the organization of collective action, and so, a poor initial stock of social capital is an obstacle to the subsequent development of more social capital. Another significant difference between the two towns worth noting here, is the distinct role of local government in promoting associations: an active role in the case of Communist-led Luco and a passive role in the case of Trasacco.

My second example relates to English craftsmen at the end of the eighteenth century and the beginning of the nineteenth century, during the early industrial revolution in England. In this example, I draw on data from E. P. Thompson's *The Making of the English Working Class*.

Between 1792 and 1796 numerous associations emerged in England demanding political reforms. The most important of these, the London Correspondence Society, was founded in January 1792, and claimed to have several thousand members a year later. This association had close links with other similar organizations, such as the Sheffield Constitutional Society (which had around 2,500 members in 1792), and similar societies in Manchester, Norwich, Bolton, Derby, Nottingham, and Coventry. New reformist societies were created in 1793 in Birmingham, Leeds, Hertfordshire, and Tewkesbury. The aim of all these societies was to secure an extension of the franchise to all adult males. Some more radical members, inspired by the Jacobin experience in France, and by Thomas Paine's *Rights of Man*, also demanded the declaration of a Republic in England and recognition of social rights for English workers (at least until the disillusionment with the Jacobins after 1793). In short all these societies pursued a public good: political reform.

The costs assumed by their members, especially the most prominent figures, were considerable. From the end of 1792 onward, the Prime Minister, Pitt, banned the publication of Paine's *Rights of Man*, and unleashed a wave of repression against political reformers. Some of the founders of the London Correspondence Society, such as Thomas Hardy and John Thelwall, were tried for treason, and many other reformists and Jacobins were deported to Australia or New Zealand.

Participation in the reformist associations in England at the end of the eighteenth century posed a social dilemma, given the public-good aim of the associations, and the high costs of participation. According to E. P. Thompson, the explanation for this radical political activity lies in the political traditions of English craftsmen. Their belief in their rights as "free-born Englishman," or support for the old Saxon free constitution—before the imposition of the "Norman yoke"—led craftsmen to fight together against the destruction of constitutional principles and the corrupt policy of parliament and the government. This, combined with the inspiration of the French Revolution and the falling living conditions due to the war with France provided the foundations for the "boom" of the reformist associations. But this is not the whole story. Constitutional values or declining living conditions may explain the preferences of many of the craftsmen, but they do not show how they overcame their social dilemma.

In fact, there were two types of English craftsmen. One group held collectivist values. As many contemporary witnesses (priests, factory inspectors, radical propagandists) observed, during critical periods (whether due to unemployment, strikes, or illness) many craftsmen helped their colleagues. These type of workers had, therefore, some kind of cooperative preferences: they were conditional cooperators, or they had the preferences of an assurance game.[2] However, other workers had more individualistic values: values of "self-help" and aristocratic aspirations. Their preferences were more like those of the prisoner's dilemma. Moreover, beyond the group of known people, it was probable that English craftsmen had incomplete information about the other workers' type. Another reason for uncertainty of this type was the possible existence of government spies operating within craftsmen's associations. Indeed, the English government frequently resorted to the use of spies. For example, "citizen Groves," a prominent member of the London Correspondence Society in 1794, was, in fact a spy of the Prime Minister Pitt (something that was never discovered by his comembers).

Given the existence of various "types" of craftsmen and the uncertainty involved, trust could have been a key element in overcoming the social dilemma. Craftsmen with preferences for an assurance game could join associations because they considered their comembers trustworthy, that is, they expected that their comembers were of the cooperative type. The origins of this trust could be diverse, but there was one main source: many members of the reformist associations had experience of participation in mutual aid societies. These mutualist societies helped craftsmen who were on strike, unemployed, or ill, but only members of the given society. At the beginning of the industrial revolution, when craftsmen began to lose customers and many of them were forced to close their shops, mutual aid societies proliferated throughout England, as a result of the absence of public social benefits. Their aim was a private good: insurance against a wide variety of risks. This insurance could only be accessed through participation in these kinds of organizations. Members of the association might have been of one of the two types already mentioned: cooperators and defectors, given that prisoner's dilemma–like preferences were not an obstacle to participation in private-good associations. But membership of mutual aid societies could provide members with information about their comembers' type: for example, their political preferences or their attitudes toward cooperation; in short, information about their trustworthiness. Although most of the members of the reform associations had previously been members of mutual societies, this was not a result of a conscious strategy by Jacobins and reformists to infiltrate mutual aid societies. Rather, it was probably due to the existence of relations of trust in those societies that could be exploited to create reformist associations.

Thus, the creation of mutual societies eased, thanks to the development of relations of trust between their members, the creation of reformist public-good oriented political associations. These new associations were a source of new relations of trust, but the generation of a virtuous circle of social capital creation was frustrated by government repression from the end of 1792. During the first decade of the nineteenth century, in the middle of the war against Napoleon, these associations all but disappeared. This was a good example of how the State can often act as a destroyer of social capital.

These two historical examples nicely illustrate how social capital can trigger a virtuous circle for the creation of more social capital. Most of the relations identified in these two examples have been considered in previous chapters: the creation of social and particularized trust as a by-product of participation in associations. In one of the stories the State plays a negative role (the repressive measures implemented by the Pitt government), and in the other an implicitly positive role (the role of the

Communist local government in Luco). In these stories we can also see how social capital created inside private-good associations can foster the creation of public-good associations. Nevertheless, two things remain to be explained about virtuous circles. First, although I have proposed in chapter five explanatory mechanisms for this relation, I have not yet tested whether participation in associations does indeed foster social trust. Second, the effects of social and particularized trust on participation in associations, even though postulated in the aforementioned examples, have not yet been explained.

I first test for both questions—that is, whether participation in private-good associations creates social trust and whether this fosters participation in associations—and then I offer explanatory mechanisms for the second of these relations, that is the relation between social trust and participation in public-good associations.

The test for this hypothesis is rather more complex than those carried out so far. I test it using a simultaneous equations model with two endogenous variables. Exogenous variables have both direct and indirect effects on endogenous variables. The use of a simultaneous equations model is justified by the presence of more than one exogenous variable, and also by the indirect effects of some variables on others. This recursive model is shown in figure 7.2.

There are two endogenous variables in the model: Y_1: social trust and Y_2: participation in public-good associations. As can be seen, social trust affects participation in public-good associations. The other variable in the model is exogenous: X_1 (participation in private-good associations) that affects Y_1 (social trust) directly and Y_2 (participation in public-good associations) indirectly. I have added three control variables: X_2 (civic norms), X_3 (educational level), and X_4 (individual income).

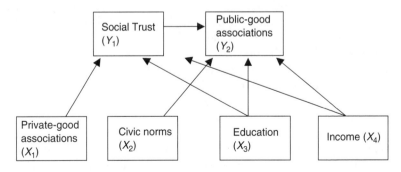

Figure 7.2   Model of the virtuous circle of social capital

My sample includes all member countries of the EU (before the current ampliation process), except Luxembourg and Greece. That is: Austria, Belgium, Denmark, Finland, France, Germany, Ireland, Italy, Netherlands, Portugal, Spain, Sweden, and the United Kingdom. The data is drawn from the 1990–91 wave of the World Value Survey. I have previously weighted the samples of these countries.

The results of the simultaneous equations model are shown in figure 7.3 and table 7.1. This shows that, after controlling for education and income, membership of private-good associations is significantly and positively linked to social trust. More specifically, it can be seen from figure 7.4 that, for the better educated and those with income levels constant around the mean, the probability of trusting unknown people is about 40–50 percent if you are not a member of a private-good association, and 90 percent if you are a member of an association. At the same time, as expected, when controlling for income, education, and civic norms, social trust is positively and significantly related to membership in public-good associations. More specifically, the probability of joining a public-good association for an individual with a high educational level and an average income is 20 percent if he does not trust other people, and 35 percent if he does trust (see figure 7.5).

These results support the hypothesis that membership of private-good associations fosters the development of public-good associations. Therefore, we can conclude that social capital creates more social capital.

Therefore, I have dealt with the first of the unexplained parts of the virtuous circle: the testing of whether participation in private-good associations leads to social trust and if social trust fosters participation in public-good associations. I now move on to explain how the

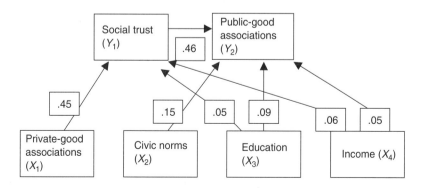

Figure 7.3 Empirical test of the model

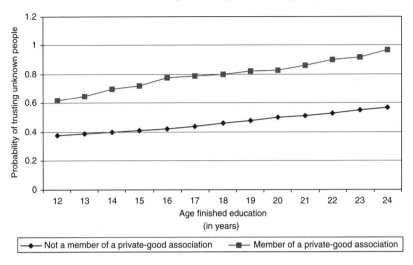

Figure 7.4   Probability of trusting unknown people

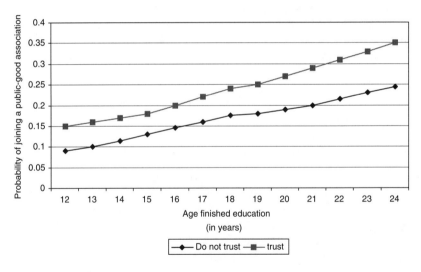

Figure 7.5   Probability of joining a public-good association

mechanisms of social trust and participation in public-good associations operate.[3]

As I noted in chapter five, in the case of private-good associations participation in the association is a necessary condition for the

Table 7.1 Simultaneous equations model

Variables	Coefficients
Social Trust	
Membership to private-good associations	0.453★★★ (0.041)
Education	0.055★★★ (0.007)
Income	0.63★★★ (0.007)
Membership of public-good associations	0.464★★★
Social trust	(0.047)
Civic norms	0.158★★★ (0.051)
Education	0.096★★★ (0.008)
Income	0.053★★★ (0.009)

Notes: Standard errors in brackets. ★★★ Significant at 99 percent.

Source: *World Value Surveys*, 1990.

attainment of the private good. That is, there is no collective-action problem. Trust plays only a minor role. If the only way to attain a certain good is to participate in a given association, I will have to participate if I want that good. The role of trust, therefore, is mainly of relevance to participation in public-good associations.

Although social capitalists repeatedly claim that social capital is, among other things, a way of resolving collective-action problems (Putnam, 1993a: 167; Kolankiewicz, 1996: 437; Taylor, 1996; Kenworthy, 1997; Minkoff, 1997: 611; Brehm and Rahn, 1997: 999–1000; Hayashi et al., 1999; Hall, 1999: 418), this often appears to be taken as an axiom without requiring further explanatory mechanisms. I now try to develop and explain these mechanisms. The final part of the chapter deals therefore, not just with the creation of social capital, as elsewhere in the book, but also, indirectly, with the effects of social capital on other variables. In fact, the impact of social capital for the resolution of collective-action problems is also responsible for influencing other variables, such as the efficiency of institutions. For example, participation in associations and their consequent positive effects for democracy also implies having previously overcome a collective-action dilemma, at least in the case of a public-good association.

In the following pages, I suggest various ways in which trust can help solve social dilemmas. Figure 7.6 serves to illustrate my arguments.

Figure 7.6 illustrates the role of trust in different situations that can lead to a social dilemma.[4] Players can be of two types: egoistic or altruistic. The egoistic player only seeks to satisfy his own interests, while the altruistic pursues the common good. Nevertheless, the altruistic player is also instrumentally rational. That is, he is a consequentialist: even if he looks for the common good, he will not choose to cooperate if he thinks he is going to be cheated. He is not an unconditional cooperator, like for example, a devotee of Kant's categorical imperative, or the *enkratés* citizen of the Greek *polis* (Domènech, 1989: 92–93). Individuals with these preferences do not need to form optimistic expectations about other people's behavior in order to cooperate, and, therefore, trust is irrelevant for them.

The highest branch of the tree shown in figure 7.6 relates to players in a prisoner's dilemma. The strategic form of this game is as follows:

	Cooperate	*Defeat*
Cooperate	*b, b*	*d, a*
Defeat	*a, d*	*c, c*

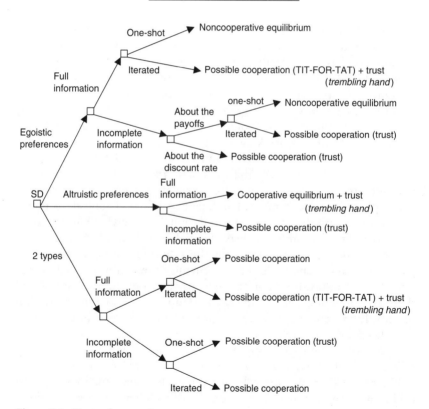

Figure 7.6   Trust and cooperation

The order of payoffs for both players is $a > b > c > d$. Trust can only play a role in an infinitely iterated prisoner's dilemma, or when neither player knows when the final round will take place. In a one-shot prisoner's dilemma, the dominant strategy of both players is noncooperation, whether or not they have full information. The common solution to the iterated prisoner's dilemma is the development of strategies of conditional cooperation. In this case, it is argued, what one player decides to do determines what the other will do next, so threats and promises—implicit or explicit—become possible. This is normally generalized in conditional strategies such as tit-for-tat: "cooperate in the first round of the game, and in the following round make the same move the other player made in the previous round" (Axelrod, 1984). If both players discount the future sufficiently, that is, if their discount rate is sufficiently high, a combination of two strategies of conditional cooperation such as tit-for-tat can be an equilibrium.[5] Nevertheless, the truth is that the resulting equilibrium of the combination of two tit-for-tat strategies is not free of problems. The main difficulty is that it is an undetermined outcome: as is demonstrated in folk theorems, many more equilibria are possible in an iterated prisoner's dilemma, among them mutual noncooperation. In fact, tit-for-tat is only the best response to another tit-for-tat strategy. A further problem is that, given the short-term costs of cooperation (the unilateral costs, i.e., the potential losses if you are the only one that cooperates), it is not clear why a player should decide to cooperate in the first place (Lange, 1991: 157; Gambetta, 1988a: 216). In any event, in a game with full information, where each player knows the other's payoffs and his discount rate, and where these are favorable to the development of strategies of cooperation like tit-for-tat, each player can assume that his best strategy is tit-for-tat, and that his opponent will think the same. In this case, contrary to the dominant view defended in the literature, I do not think that trust has an important role to play. At best, trust can eliminate the threat that the likelihood of trembling hands poses for a cooperative outcome. Trembling hands (Rasmusen, 1989: 27) do not necessarily refer to irrational movements, but to mistakes by some players in their strategy. As I have noted, with full information, and under certain circumstances, both players may choose a tit-for-tat strategy. But, under these same circumstances, there is still the likelihood of a trembling hand, that is, of a mistake being made in implementing the strategy. In an iterated prisoner's dilemma, in which the cost of being a sucker in one of the rounds is disproportionately high, even if the likelihood of a trembling hand is very low, a player can opt to not cooperate. If the subjective probability of a trembling hand is 0, because you trust your partner, cooperation will not be disrupted, for example, by confidence in the other player's ability to perform a certain task, or in his powers of concentration.

The role of trust is potentially higher if we assume incomplete information. As can be seen in figure 7.6, when the prisoner's dilemma is one-shot, the outcome once more is noncooperation. However, more possibilities are opened up in an iterated game. In this case, tit-for-tat is once more a possible strategy for both players, but, given that now they do not know the payoffs of the other player, or their discount rate, or both, each of them is unsure about the other's strategy. One player can form subjective probabilities about the discount rate or the payoffs for the other. Under certain circumstances, this could lead one to cooperation. For example, if a player decides that the payoffs or discount rate of the other favor tit-for-tat, it is possible that she will also decide to opt for tit-for-tat (if she discounts the future sufficiently, or her potential costs are not very high (Kydd, 2000)). But it is also possible that she will choose to cooperate initially in order to cheat a tit-for-tat player. In fact, it is not necessary to be a conditional cooperator in order to cooperate in the first round. One only has to be sophisticated enough to cheat. In Hargreaves and Varoufakis's game (1995: 179–182) between two egoistic players with incomplete information, but who know that the other is a conditional cooperator, both will cooperate at least in $t = 1$, even though the game is finite and the number of rounds is known. Each may believe that their initial cooperative behavior permits the Bayesian updating of the prior expectations of the other player, and that the other player will take their cooperative move as a signal of future behavior (Burt and Knez, 1995: 258; Lahno, 1995). By these means, she will hope to cheat her partner.

Therefore, trust plays a marginal role in the solution of an iterated prisoner's dilemma with full information, but may play an important role if there is incomplete information.

The central branch of the figure 7.6 tree leads to another type of game. In this case, these are coordination games. In these games, both players are altruistic. In fact, they would be something like consequentialist cooperators. They are not, as I have already said, unconditional cooperators in a Kantian sense. They could, for example, be Martin Hollis's (1998: 162) "reasonable" individuals, partly Kantian unconditional cooperators, and partly individuals that use general reciprocity. These players will prefer an outcome of mutual cooperation, but if the other does not cooperate, they will prefer not to cooperate. Additionally, they prefer an outcome in which they do not cooperate and the other cooperates to one in which they are the suckers, cooperating when the other defeats them The strategic form of this assurance game is as follows:

The order of the payoffs for both players is $a > b > c > d$. The two equilibria in pure strategies are cooperate–cooperate and defeat–defeat.

	Cooperate	Defeat
Cooperate	a, a	d, c
Defeat	c, d	b, b

With full information, a simple way to select an equilibrium is to consider that the outcome of the game is a Pareto-optimum equilibrium, that is, the equilibrium of mutual cooperation. This is, for example, Michael Taylor's solution (Taylor, 1987: 39). It is assumed that the coordination of both players in this solution is easy: they simply have to communicate. This form of coordination can be dangerous, however, if there are major differences in the payoffs. In the order of payoffs in the aforementioned matrix, a is higher than d. This only reflects the ordinal preferences of the players, but not its intensity. Suppose that d (the payoff when one player cooperates and the other decides not to cooperate), is extremely low, so that the consequences of the other's nonfulfillment of the agreement is serious. Once more, trust plays a minor role in the cooperative solution to this game, and only after we reintroduce the notion of trembling hand. Strong expectations about the professionalism, or powers of concentration of the other player can result in neither of the players thinking about the probability of trembling hands. Suppose, for example, that various peasants create an association to build a dike that is essential for the irrigation of their plots. Individually, none of them can build the dike: all of them are needed. The two equilibria of this game in pure strategies are that everybody cooperates in the building of the dike, or nobody does. The best equilibrium is the second one, and, in principle, peasants can come to this equilibrium simply by talking about it. Nevertheless, each peasant might also think that there is a small probability of some members of the association not playing their part, for whatever reason (e.g., because they forget, or because they begin to think that the water gods disapprove of dikes). Such an outcome can be discarded if the peasants trust (correctly or not) in the professionalism of the other members (their confidence might derive, e.g., from their knowledge of each other).

Once more, it is likely that trust will play a more important role if there is not full information. In this case, although both players are cooperators, they do not know each other's payoffs. Or, if they do know each other's payoffs, they do not know if the other player knows the first player's payoffs. Even though I know that the other player is a cooperator, I am not sure that he knows that I am also a cooperator, in which case it is possible that he will opt to not cooperate (given that I am a nonconsequentialist cooperator). To illustrate this, I use the example of the dilemma facing the European social democratic parties in 1914. In 1914, social democracy faced one of its most traumatic decisions in history. Parties committed to maintaining peace finally voted in favor of war credits in their respective national parliaments, decisions that split the II International asunder. We can suggest various explanations for this vote. One possible explanation is that although the social democratic parties opposed war, they did not know how to avoid it, beyond some vague notions of a "general strike at the international level" (as discussed at the SFIO's (French Section of the Workers' International) Congress held on July 15–16, 1914 (Rebérioux, 1985: 791) or the Stuttgart Congress of the II International in 1907 (Sasson, 1997: 27)). Other less benign interpretations relate to the preferences of the leaders of the social democratic parties. For example, Lenin (1974, 1980) argued that the bourgeoisie used the surplus profits derived from imperialism to bribe labor leaders. Although he did not mean that individual socialist leaders were directly bribed by the capitalists, some of his claims in *Imperialism. The Highest Stage of Capitalism*, or in the article "Imperialism and the Split of Socialism" do point in that direction. However, I would like to suggest a rather different explanation: socialist leaders faced a coordination game with asymmetric information. Let us begin by making a reasonable assumption: that the socialist parties were initially against war. Let us further suppose that they knew how to stop the war. This assumption is less plausible, as the idea of an international general strike seems scarcely credible coming from such an important organization as the International. However, it is not necessary to assume that an international general strike was in fact an effective means of preventing war. It is sufficient to believe that the leaders of the main parties believed it to be so. This assumption is not so restrictive. On the basis of these two assumptions, we can identify the two main players: the French Section of the International (SFIO) and the German Social Democratic Party (SPD). The first preference of both organizations was a joint vote against war credits. Such a vote would not merely be a symbolic act, but a necessary first step in implementing other measures to stop war, such as the international general strike. However, if one of the parties decided to vote in favor of war credits, the others would prefer to do the same. The reason is that if one of them voted in favor of war, the measures against war could not be put into effect. Voting unilaterally against war credits only had costs for the party concerned, such as exposure to charges of national disloyalty or being declared illegal. Therefore, the structure of the game between the SFIO and the SPD is that of a coordination game with incomplete information, with two possible equilibria in pure form: a joint vote in favor of war credits or a joint vote against them. Incomplete information surrounded the preferences of both parties. That is, it is possible that neither party were sure about the other's preferences, whether they were for or against the war. However I do not think this was in fact that case. The uncertainty mainly derived from the fact that, although both were sure about the other's preferences (both thought that the other was pacifist) they were not sure that the other party knew that they were also against war. That is, although both thought that they were involved in a coordination game, both were not sure if the other thought that their preferences were those of a prisoner's dilemma. Equally, both were afraid of the occurrence of "trembling hands," especially considering the cost of voting unilaterally against war. Nevertheless, they made some efforts to coordinate in a joint negative vote equilibrium. Before the vote the SPD sent an emissary, Hermann Müller, to seek French support for a joint vote against war credits (Kirby, 1986: 28–29), but the SFIO's leaders did not believe his word. Therefore, the vote of workers' parties in favor of war credits was largely due to a problem of coordination. The origin of the problem lay in one player's uncertainty about the other's type, the fear of trembling hands, and the lack of trust between both parties about both these issues (Herreros, 2003).

In the lower branches of the tree in figure 7.6, we have games between two types of players: consequentialist cooperators and players with prisoner's dilemma preferences. If we assume that in a particular population there are players of both types, when the game is between two consequentialist cooperators, we return to the central branches of figure 7.6. In this case, as I have already pointed out, it is possible that cooperation in a one-shot game. If the game is between a consequentialist cooperator and a player with prisoner's dilemma's preferences, the outcome would be different. The strategic form of this game is as follows:

	Cooperate	Defeat
Cooperate	a, b	d, a
Defeat	c, d	b, c

As in the previous matrixes, the order of payoffs for both players is $a > b > c > d$. The only equilibrium in pure strategies of this game is that both lose. It is the same in the prisoner's dilemma: a game of this type played once and with full information leads to a noncooperative equilibrium. With incomplete information, trust can once again play a role. This is the case, for example, in a one-shot game in which neither of the players know the other's type. If at least one of them is a consequentialist cooperator, his decision to cooperate will mainly depend on his expectations about the type of the other player. That is, on his confidence in the other also being a consequentialist cooperator. If both are cooperators and trusters, the outcome will be mutual cooperation. If only one of them is a cooperator, and he mistakenly trusts in the other's trustworthiness, he will be miserably cheated. Trust, therefore, helps the attainment of cooperative equilibria only if both players are cooperators. If they are not, it is a sure way of being cheated.

In an iterated game, trust, once more, will play a minor role if there is full information. If players are conditional cooperators, it is obvious that the outcome of the game will be a combination of tit-for-tat strategies. In any case, trust can play a role in the possibility of trembling hands, for reasons pointed out before. If only one player is a conditional cooperator, noncooperation will be the strategy adopted by both.

Trust can play a more significant role in repeated games with incomplete information. When neither of the players knows the other's type, new possibilities are opened up. A conditional cooperator, if he has sufficient trust in the other player also being a conditional cooperator, can begin cooperating. If the other reciprocates, the outcome can be mutual cooperation. If the other player is an opportunist, he has various options if he thinks he is faced with a conditional cooperator. If he sufficiently discounts future payoffs and he thinks that the consequentialist cooperator will not be exploited beyond the first round, then he can opt to play tit-for-tat. Or he can start cooperating to induce the other player into thinking that he is a conditional cooperator, and then cheat him in the future.

To sum up, if two types of players relate randomly, trust will play a role where there is incomplete information. In a one-shot game or an iterated game, an opportunistic player who thinks that the other player is a conditional cooperator can try to exploit him by pretending for a while to be a cooperator. In this case, the trust displayed by the consequentialist cooperator about the other's player type favors a cooperative outcome only in the event of the other player also being a cooperator. Otherwise, trust favors the exploitation of the truster by opportunistic players.

In these cases, the consequentialist cooperator should follow Machiavelli's maxim: "a man that wants to be good in all situations will be ruined among many bad" (Machiavelli, 1992: 83).

To conclude, trust can play a role in the solution of certain social dilemmas. In social dilemmas with complete information, trust plays a minor role. Both in the prisoner's dilemma and in the assurance game, and also in the game between the consequentialist cooperator and the egoistic player, trust's possible role is to reduce the fear of the occurrence of trembling hands. However, if incomplete information is introduced, the role of trust becomes more important in all the social dilemmas considered.

Analyzing the role of trust in participation in associations, the story of the "virtuous circle" in the creation of social capital is closed. Now, our own circle is also closed: we have answered the question of why some communities are blessed with higher levels of social capital than others. I have shown how, under certain circumstances, social capital can be the source of more social capital. If initial differences exist in terms of social capital, explained, for example, by the different role or attitude of the State, these differences can perpetuate themselves over time, because more social capital generates even more social capital. The good news is that this process is not irreversible. As I have tried to demonstrate over the course of this book, there are many ways of setting out to create social capital.

CHAPTER EIGHT

Conclusions

I began the introduction to this book with a critique of the social capital research program. I said, on the one hand, that social capital was ill defined, and, on the other, that we do not understand clearly how to invest in social capital. In fact neither of these criticisms are surprising, given that it is an extremely delicate form of capital, and, thus, difficult to define. My underlying task was to analyze what factors account for the differences in social capital between communities. The social capital literature has demonstrated, sometimes very convincingly, the positive effects that social capital can produce for the wider society. However, it has not been able to explain the difference in social capital between, say, Spain and Sweden. This is an important topic, given the apparently immense possibilities of this resource.

In this book, I have tried to explain what lies behind these differences. I have argued that the role of the State is crucial for the development of social capital, through its role as a guarantor of agreements and through its potentially positive role in the formation of voluntary associations. Difference in the role of the State across countries could explain initial differences in social capital. Moreover, what is equally important, the State's action could put in motion a "virtuous circle" of the creation of social capital, as I have tried to demonstrate in chapter 7. This means that social capital creates more social capital. The consequence is that initial difference in the stock of social capital across nations will become higher over time. Nevertheless, this is not to say that countries or communities with low levels of social capital are condemned to remain in their miserable situation. One of the positive things about the analysis of the role of the State in the creation of social capital is that it points out a way to escape from the gloomy destiny of eternal scarcity of social capital. This is an original conclusion, given that it has traditionally been assumed that "more State means less social capital." In this work I have advanced theoretical as well as empirical arguments to support my claim that the State can play a positive role in the generation of social capital.

Apart from this general argument that structures the book, I hope to have made significant contributions in at least in two areas: the definition of social capital and the mechanisms that link social networks to relations of trust.

In chapter 2, I offered a definition of social capital that seeks to connect membership of social networks with the resources derived from it. Social capital, I have argued, is an obligation of reciprocity linked to a relation of trust and information associated with membership of social networks. Even though the study of attitudes, values, and social norms might be interesting in an analysis of the development of expectations of trust, attitudes and values do not themselves constitute social capital. The definition I have put forward suggests social capital may be created as a by-product of other activities, but also that it can be created intentionally, as the result of a conscious decision to invest in it. You can be a member of an association, for example, exclusively for the personal contacts it offers.

It is usually assumed that trust, social as well as particularized, is created as a by-product of participation in social networks. However, explanations about how these mechanisms operate are systematically absent from the literature. Here I have outlined some of these mechanisms, as well as some alternative ways that social capital can be created. Indirectly, the arguments developed in chapters 4–7 may help clarify a third issue: the analysis of trust from a rational choice perspective. It is occasionally suggested that individuals who are too rational cannot trust others. I do not agree. Everything depends on the information individuals collate to form their expectations. In the case of particularized trust, beliefs are easily rational. It is relatively easy to gather information, given that you know the preferences of the other as a by-product of past experiences with her. In the case of social trust, this information is much more difficult to obtain. You do not now the other, by definition, and you have to deal with this uncertainty. Once more, the rationality of expectations depends on the information collected. If you gather all the relevant information about this stranger (asking his friends, or his foes, e.g.) your expectations may be perfectly rational and you can trust, if the information collected indicates that he is a trustworthy individual. If you base your expectation on various types of heuristics or shortcuts (the Vietnamese peasants using external signals is one example of this) then the situation is not quite as clear, but it is debatable whether or not these expectations are rational. As I stated in the introduction, and as Popkin (1991) claims, the use of these heuristics would be rational if it leads to the same conclusion had the individual collated all the relevant information.

Even though all these arguments relate to the formation of social capital, they also have implications for the study of the effects of social capital on other variables. Consider, for example, the relation between social capital and democratic governance. This relation has been analyzed from different perspectives since Putnam's original study of regional governments in Italy. In order to introduce a new perspective, at least one that is new to the social capital literature, I refer here to the recent debate about "associative democracy." Paul Hirst has been one of the most recent contributors to this debate. Among other things, he maintains that an increase in the power and responsibility of associations should be accompanied by a decrease in the responsibilities of the State. Other proponents of associative democracy, notably Joshua Cohen and Joel Rogers, argue that the State should play an active role in promoting associationism. Both proposals consider that these associations should be democratically organized. Does the social capital school have anything to contribute to this debate about associative democracy? Undoubtedly, there are common points between both research programs. For example, according to the defenders of associative democracy, some of the mechanisms that link an active role inside associations with more democratic government, can be equally useful when looking at the benefits of social capital for democracy. Among other things, both traditions argue that participation in associations generates more information about politicians' behavior and that this, at the same time, favors greater democratic accountability. As for the role of the State or associations' internal organization, research into social capital could provide new points of view. The results of my work suggest there are good grounds to back Cohen and Rogers's proposal. The State can actively support the development of new associations, through for example, the Welfare State. Once created inside associations, social capital can generate unexpected benefits for democracy; improved economic performance for example. At the same time, the conclusions provide new arguments to defend the democratic nature of the working of associations. Internal democracy can be defended simply on the grounds of democratic principles (as Dahl (1985) does e.g., when defending industrial democracy), or by the beneficial effects internal democracy has for society as a whole. For example, more democratic political parties provide citizens with more political information (Maravall, 1999). From the point of view of social capital, and in light of the conclusions of this book, the democratic organization of associations can equally well be justified by their greater capacity to generate social capital. The development of relations of trust is, for the reasons outlined in the chapter 4, easier in horizontal and democratic organizations than in vertical ones.

In Andrei Platonov's (1927) novel *Chevengur*, Chepurni, one of the leaders of Chevengur's amazing commune says that in a Communist society the only capital left would be one's friends. Unfortunately, we cannot share Chepurni's confidence in the final triumph of social capital. Nevertheless, the conclusions drawn over the course of this book allow us to view the social capital research program more optimistically. It is possible to define a significant third form of capital, which is not merely trust or participation in associations. It is also possible to invest in this form of capital. What remains to be seen, perhaps, is whether it is indeed worth investing in.

Appendix: Coding

Participation in Associations and Particularized Trust

The coding of the variables of table 4.1 is the following:

Particularized trust. Source: *Barómetro de Opinión Pública de Andalucía (IESAA/CSIC)* [Barometer of Andalusian Public Opinion 2000]. *Text of the question:* "Generally speaking, how much do you trust the co-members of your association? Much; Quite; Nothing." *Coding:* value 1 if they say much or quite, value 0 otherwise.

Horizontal associations. Source: *Barómetro de Opinión Pública de Andalucía (IESAA/CSIC)* [Barometer of Andalusian Public Opinion 2000]. *Text of the question:* "When decisions are adopted inside your association, how many of the members participate in the decision making-process? Most decisions are taken just by a few members of the association; Most decisions are taken with the participation of most of the members of the associations." *Coding:* value 1 if decisions are adopted by most of the members, value 0 otherwise.

Education. Source: *Barómetro de Opinión Pública de Andalucía (IESAA/CSIC)* [Barometer of Andalusian Public Opinion 2000]. *Text of the question:* "What are the higher-level studies you have finished?" *Coding:* ordinal variable with range 1–6, 1 being the lower level of education and 6 the higher.

Income. Source: *Barómetro de Opinión Pública de Andalucía (IESAA/CSIC)* [Barometer of Andalusian Public Opinion 2000]. *Text of the question:* "Finally, could you say me what are your current income?" *Coding:* ordinal variable with range 1–12, 1 being the lower level of education and 12 the higher.

The State and the Creation of Social Capital

The coding of the variables of table 6.3 is the following:

Corruption. Source: Transparency International 1995.

Trust. Source: World Value Surveys 1990–91. *Text of the question:* "Generally speaking would you say that most people can be trusted or that you can't be too careful in dealing with people?" *Coding:* value 1 for those who say that most people can be trusted, 0 otherwise.

Capitalists, small employers, petty bourgeoisie, new middle class, working class. Source: World Value Surveys 1990–91. *Text of the question:* "What is/was your job there? Employer/manager of establishment with ten or more employees; Employer/manager of establishment with less than ten employees; professional worker lawyer, accountant, teacher; middle level non-manual office worker; junior non-manual office worker; foreman and supervisor; skilled manual worker; semi-skilled manual worker; unskilled manual worker; farmer: employer, or manager on own account; agricultural worker." *Coding*: employer with ten or more employees: capitalists (value 5); employer with less than ten employees: small employers (value 4); farmer: employer or manager on own account: petty bourgeoisie (value 3); professional worker lawyer, accountant, teacher, middle-level non-manual office worker, junior non-manual office worker, skilled manual worker, foreman, and supervisor: new middle class (value 2); semi-skilled manual worker; unskilled manual worker: working class (category of reference. Value 1).

Political interest. Source: World Value Surveys 1990–91. *Text of the question*: "How interested would you say you are in politics?" *Coding*: ordinal variable.

Education. Source: World Value Surveys 1990–91. *Text of the question*: "School-leaving Age." *Coding*: ordinal variable.

Income. Source: World Value Surveys 1990–91. *Text of the question*: "Here is a scale of incomes. We would like to know in what group your household is, counting all wages, salaries, pensions and other incomes that come in. Just give the letter of the group your household falls into, before taxes and other deductions." *Coding*: ordinal variable.

Church assistance. Source: World Value Surveys 1990–91. *Text of the question*: "Apart from weddings, funerals and christenings, about how often do you attend religious services these days?" *Coding*: ordinal variable.

Associational membership. Source: World Value Surveys 1990–91. *Text of the question*: "Please look carefully at the following list of voluntary organizations and activities and say which, if any, do you belong to? Social welfare services for elderly, handicapped or deprived people; Religious or church organizations; Education, arts, music or cultural activities; trade unions; political parties or groups; local community actions in issues like poverty, employment, housing, racial equality; third world development or human rights; conservation, the environment, ecology; professional associations; youth work; sports or recreation; women's groups; peace movements; animal rights; voluntary organizations concerned with health; other groups." *Coding*: value 1, member of any of the associations; value 0, not member of an association.

The coding of the variables of table 6.6 is the following:

Associational membership. Source: World Value Surveys 1990–91. *Text of the question*: "Please look carefully at the following list of voluntary organizations and activities and say which, if any, do you belong to? Social welfare services for elderly, handicapped or deprived people; Religious or church organizations; Education, arts, music or cultural activities; trade unions; political parties or groups; local community actions in issues like poverty, employment, housing, racial equality; third world development or human rights; conservation, the environment, ecology; professional associations; youth work; sports or recreation; women's groups; peace movements; animal rights; voluntary organizations concerned with health; other groups." *Coding*: value 1, member of any of the associations; value 0, not member of an association.

Expenditure. Source: European Commission, OECD, World Bank Development Indicators (1999).

Education. Source: World Value Surveys 1990–91. *Text of the question*: "School-leaving Age." *Coding*: ordinal variable.

Capitalists, small employers, petty bourgeoisie, new middle class, working class. Source: World Value Surveys 1990–91. *Text of the question*: "What is/was your job there? Employer/manager of establishment with ten or more employees; Employer/manager of establishment with less than ten employees; professional worker lawyer, accountant, teacher; middle level non-manual office worker; junior non-manual office worker; foreman and supervisor; skilled manual worker; semi-skilled manual worker; unskilled manual worker; farmer: employer manager on own account; agricultural worker." *Coding*: employer with ten or more employees, employer with less than ten employees: capitalists (value 4: category of reference); farmer: employer, or manager on own account: petty bourgeoisie (value 3); professional worker lawyer, accountant, teacher, middle-level non-manual office worker, junior non-manual office worker, skilled manual worker, foreman and supervisor: new middle class (value 2); semi-skilled manual worker; unskilled manual worker: working class (category of reference. Value 1).

City. Source: World Value Surveys 1990–91. *Text of the question:* "Size of town." *Coding:* ordinal variable.

Trust. Source: World Value Surveys 1990–91. *Text of the question:* "Generally speaking would you say that most people can be trusted or that you can't be too careful in dealing with people?" *Coding:* value 1 for those who say that most people can be trusted, 0 otherwise.

The coding of the variables of table 6.7 is the following:

Associational membership. Source: World Value Surveys 1990–91. *Text of the question:* "Please look carefully at the following list of voluntary organizations and activities and say which, if any, do you belong to? Social welfare services for elderly, handicapped or deprived people; Religious or church organizations; Education, arts, music or cultural activities; trade unions; political parties or groups; local community actions in issues like poverty, employment, housing, racial equality; third world development or human rights; conservation, the environment, ecology; professional associations; youth work; sports or recreation; women's groups; peace movements; animal rights; voluntary organizations concerned with health; other groups." *Coding:* value 1, member of any of the associations; value 0, not member of an association.

Expenditure. Source: European Commission, OECD, World Bank Development Indicators (1999).

Education. Source: World Value Surveys 1990–91. *Text of the question:* "School-leaving Age." *Coding:* ordinal variable.

Capitalists, small employers, petty bourgeoisie, new middle class, working class. Source: World Value Surveys 1990–91. *Text of the question:* "What is/was your job there? Employer/manager of establishment with ten or more employees; Employer/manager of establishment with less than ten employees; professional worker lawyer, accountant, teacher; middle level non-manual office worker; junior non-manual office worker; foreman and supervisor; skilled manual worker; semi-skilled manual worker; unskilled manual worker; farmer: employer manager on own account; agricultural worker." *Coding:* employer with ten or more employees, employer with less than ten employees: capitalists (value 4: category of reference); farmer: employer or manager on own account: petty bourgeoisie (value 3); professional worker lawyer, accountant, teacher, middle-level non-manual office worker, junior non-manual office worker, skilled manual worker, foreman and supervisor: new middle class (value 2); semi-skilled manual worker; unskilled manual worker: working class (category of reference. Value 1).

City. Source: World Value Surveys 1990–91. *Text of the question:* "Size of town." *Coding:* ordinal variable.

Trust. Source: World Value Surveys 1990–91. *Text of the question:* "Generally speaking would you say that most people can be trusted or that you can't be too careful in dealing with people?" *Coding:* value 1 for those who say that most people can be trusted, 0 otherwise.

The coding of tables 6.9, 6.10, and 6.11 is as follows:

Trust. Source: World Value Surveys 1990–91. *Text of the question:* "Generally speaking would you say that most people can be trusted or that you can't be too careful in dealing with people?" *Coding:* value 1 for those who say that most people can be trusted, 0 otherwise.

Capitalists, small employers, petty bourgeoisie, new middle class, working class. Source: World Value Surveys 1990–91. *Text of the question:* "What is/was your job there? Employer/manager of establishment with ten or more employees; Employer/manager of establishment with less than ten employees; professional worker lawyer, accountant, teacher; middle level non-manual office worker; junior non-manual office worker; foreman and supervisor; skilled manual worker; semi-skilled manual worker; unskilled manual worker; farmer: employer manager on own account; agricultural worker."

Coding: employer with ten or more employees: capitalists (value 5); employer with less than ten employees: small employers (value 4); farmer: employer or manager on own account: petty bourgeoisie (value 3); professional worker lawyer, accountant, teacher, middle-level non-manual office worker, junior non-manual office worker, skilled manual worker, foreman and supervisor: new middle class (value 2); semi-skilled manual worker; unskilled manual worker: working class (category of reference. Value 1).

Political interest.   Source: World Value Surveys 1990–91. *Text of the question*: "How interested would you say you are in politics?" *Coding*: ordinal variable.

Ideology.   Source: World Value Surveys 1990–91. *Text of the question*: "In political matters, people talk of 'the left' and 'the right': How would you place your views on this scale generally speaking." *Coding*: ordinal variable.

Church assistance.   Source: World Value Surveys 1990–91. *Text of the question*: "Apart from weddings, funerals and christenings, about how often do you attend religious services these days?" *Coding*: ordinal variable.

City.   Source: World Value Surveys 1990–91. *Text of the question*: "Size of town." *Coding*: ordinal variable.

Age.   Source: World Value Surveys 1990–91. *Text of the question*: "You are … years old." *Coding*: continuous variable.

Gender.   Source: World Value Surveys 1990–91. *Text of the question*: "Sex of respondent." *Coding*: value 1, men; value 2, women.

The Virtuous Circle of the Creation of Social Capital

The coding of the variables of table 7.1 is the following:

Trust.   Source: World Value Surveys 1990–91. *Text of the question*: "Generally speaking would you say that most people can be trusted or that you can't be too careful in dealing with people?" *Coding*: value 1 for those who say that most people can be trusted, 0 otherwise.

Membership to private-good associations, membership to public-good associations.   Source: World Value Surveys 1990–91. *Text of the question*: "Please look carefully at the following list of voluntary organizations and activities and say which, if any, do you belong to? Social welfare services for elderly, handicapped or deprived people; Religious or church organizations; Education, arts, music or cultural activities; trade unions; political parties or groups; local community actions in issues like poverty, employment, housing, racial equality; third world development or human rights; conservation, the environment, ecology; professional associations; youth work; sports or recreation; women's groups; peace movements; animal rights; voluntary organizations concerned with health; other groups." *Coding*: public-goods associations: trade unions, political parties, local community action, third world development, the environment, peace movements, animal rights; the other, private-goods associations.

Civic Norms.   Source: World Value Surveys 1990–91. *Text of the question*: "Please tell me for each of the following statements whether you think it can always be justified, never justified, or something in between, using this card. Claiming government benefits to which you are not entitled; Avoiding a fare on public transport; Cheating on taxes if you have a chance; Buying something you knew was stolen; Someone accepting a bribe in the course of their duties." *Coding*: In each question, the interviewers should place themselves in a scale from 1 to 10, where 1 means that it is never justified and 10 that it is always justified. For the statistical analysis, I have built a dichotomous variable. In value 1, referred to the fulfillment of the civic norms, I include all the individuals that have placed themselves in value 1 of the scale in the five questions. In value 0, I include all the individuals that have placed themselves in a value other than 1 in at least one of the five questions.

Education. Source: World Value Surveys 1990–91. *Text of the question:* "School-leaving Age." *Coding:* ordinal variable.

Income. Source: World Value Surveys 1990–91. *Text of the question:* "Here is a scale of incomes. We would like to know in what group your household is, counting all wages, salaries, pensions and other incomes that come in. Just give the letter of the group your household falls into, before taxes and other deductions." *Coding:* ordinal variable.

The Type and the Number of Associations and Social Trust

The coding of the variables of table 5.1 is the following:

Social trust. Source: *Barómetro de Opinión Pública de Andalucía (IESAA/CSIC)* [Barometer of Andalusian Public Opinion 2000]. *Text of the question:* "Generally speaking would you say that most people can be trusted or that you can't be too careful in dealing with people?" *Coding:* value 1 for those who say that most people can be trusted, 0 otherwise.

Political associations. Source: *Barómetro de Opinión Pública de Andalucía (IESAA/CSIC)* [Barometer of Andalusian Public Opinion 2000]. *Text of the question:* "I am going to present you a list of voluntary organizations. Could you tell me if you are an active member, an inactive one, or if you are not a member of each of them? Religious associations; sports associations; unions; political parties; professional associations; environmental organizations; self-help groups; house-wife associations; feminists associations; parents associations; employers organizations; cultural, arts or musical associations, organizations for the help of ancient people, associations against poverty, students associations, any other type of associations." *Coding:* value 1 for those members of unions, political parties, environmental organizations and feminist associations, value 0 for the members of other types of associations.

Income. Source: *Barómetro de Opinión Pública de Andalucía (IESAA/CSIC)* [Barometer of Andalusian Public Opinion 2000]. *Text of the question:* "Finally, could you say me what are your current income?" *Coding:* ordinal variable with range 1–12, 1 being the lower level of education and 12 the higher.

Age. Source: *Barómetro de Opinión Pública de Andalucía (IESAA/CSIC)* [Barometer of Andalusian Public Opinion 2000]. *Text of the question:* "How many years old were you in your last birthday?" *Coding:* continuous variable.

The coding of the variables of table 5.2 is the following:

Social trust. Source: *Barómetro de Opinión Pública de Andalucía (IESAA/CSIC)* [Barometer of Andalusian Public Opinion 2000]. *Text of the question:* "Generally speaking would you say that most people can be trusted or that you can't be too careful in dealing with people?" *Coding:* value 1 for those who say that most people can be trusted, 0 otherwise.

Membership to one association. Source: *Barómetro de Opinión Pública de Andalucía (IESAA/CSIC)* [Barometer of Andalusian Public Opinion 2000]. *Text of the question:* "I am going to present you a list of voluntary organizations. Could you tell me if you are an active member, an inactive one, or if you are not a member of each of them? Religious associations; sports associations; unions; political parties; professional associations; environmental organizations; self-help groups; house-wife associations; feminists associations; parents associations; employers organizations; cultural, arts or musical associations, organizations for the help of ancient people, associations against poverty, students associations, any other type of associations." *Coding:* value 1: member of one association, value 0 otherwise.

Membership to two associations. Source: *Barómetro de Opinión Pública de Andalucía (IESAA/CSIC)* [Barometer of Andalusian Public Opinion 2000]. *Text of the question:* "I am going to present you a list of voluntary organizations. Could you tell me if you are an active member, an inactive one, or if you are not a member of each of them? Religious associations; sports associations; unions; political parties; professional associations; environmental organizations; self-help groups; house-wife associations; feminists associations; parents associations; employers organizations; cultural, arts or musical associations, organizations for the help of ancient people, associations against poverty, students associations, any other type of associations." *Coding*: value 1: member of two associations, value 0 otherwise.

Membership to three associations. Source: *Barómetro de Opinión Pública de Andalucía (IESAA/CSIC)* [Barometer of Andalusian Public Opinion 2000]. *Text of the question*: "I am going to present you a list of voluntary organizations. Could you tell me if you are an active member, an inactive one, or if you are not a member of each of them? Religious associations; sports associations; unions; political parties; professional associations; environmental organizations; self-help groups; house-wife associations; feminists associations; parents associations; employers organizations; cultural, arts or musical associations, organizations for the help of ancient people, associations against poverty, students associations, any other type of associations." *Coding*: value 1: member of three associations, value 0 otherwise.

Income. Source: *Barómetro de Opinión Pública de Andalucía (IESAA/CSIC)* [Barometer of Andalusian Public Opinion 2000]. *Text of the question*: "Finally, could you say me what are your current income?" *Coding*: ordinal variable with range 1–12, 1 being the lower level of education and 12 the higher.

Education. Source: *Barómetro de Opinión Pública de Andalucía (IESAA/CSIC)* [Barometer of Andalusian Public Opinion 2000]. *Text of the question*: "What are the higher-level studies you have finished?" *Coding*: ordinal variable with range 1–6, 1 being the lower level of education and 6 the higher.

Notes

Chapter Two   The Concept of Social Capital

1. In the literature on trust, however, we could go as far back as Niklas Luhmann, who in the early 1970s mentioned trust as a form of capital (Luhmann, 1979: 64).
2. According to James Coleman, a system of trust is a relation between two actors in which the first one trusts the second and is, at the same time, the second one's trustee. The difference between this and a simple relation of trust is that the potential losses derived from breaking the relation are greater in systems of trust and, therefore, so too are the expectations of reciprocity (Coleman, 1990: 177).
3. This example is not as extravagant as it may at first appear. In fact, John Dunn (1993) argues that one of the differences between the seventeenth- and eighteenth-century natural law philosophers and contemporary contractualists is the importance the former attach to *fides* and trust as a fundamental aspect of social life.
4. Some experiments about deliberation in groups have shown that participants learn from the deliberative process, that they often change their preferences, and that it does not seem that they modify them strategically (Fishkin and Luskin, 2000). Nevertheless, in these experiments the substantive conclusions reached in the deliberative process did not have any real application, so the incentives for the misrepresentation of revealing preferences were lower.

Chapter Three   The Problem of the Formation of Social Capital

1. Nevertheless, the reputation argument has its limits. As noted by Leibenstein (1987), in order to be effective, the belief must be based on the assumption that the information available to unsatisfied customers can easily be extended to future buyers. In many cases, this is not the case, because the process of gathering and processing relevant information is much too costly.

Chapter Four   The Creation of Particularized Trust

1. Some experimental games confirm this idea: if there is nonopportunistic behavior by one of the players, the other player assumes that he is trustworthy, and he chooses to reciprocate (Gautschi, 2000: 142).

2. Of course, not everybody would agree with that. For example, the walrasian economic model just recognized one type of power to the owners of the means of production: higher purchase power (Bowles and Gintins, 1990: 174). The Marxist view would also be rejected by the social exchange theorists' view of power: according to them, the power relations are not governed by coercion, but by the same laws that govern economic exchange (Emerson, 1962).

Chapter Five   The Creation of Social Trust

1. This example presented by Coleman sounds now somewhat inadequate. Now we cannot claim that the streets of Jerusalem are surer than the streets of Detroit. However, we could simply substitute "Jerusalem" by "Stockholm" and the example will have sense once more.
2. This kind of trust seems so implausible that, according to Geoffrey Hawthorn (1988), it is just possible in an aristocratic society, characterized by the presence of a code of "virtue and honor." Machiavelli (1996: 63) suggested a very similar idea when he argued that the function of religion in ancient Rome was to guarantee the fulfillment of agreements.
3. In fact, it is difficult for these kinds of beliefs to fulfill the requisite of consistency within a strict theory of rationality. According to Elster (1983), the consistency of beliefs requires, among other things, being in accordance with the laws of probability.
4. Even though Putnam considers that certain types of associations, the vertical ones, are not prone to the development of civic virtue, he also considers that the development of these virtues is independent of the aim of the association: it does not matter if the association is political or not.
5. There is another way in which participation in a social network my have an impact on the decision to trust. According to Becker and Murphy (2000), personal interactions influence choices and behavior, changing the individual's utilities of goods. The individual utility function would therefore be $U = U (x; y; S)$, where x and y would be goods and services, and the variable S would represent the social influences on utility through the reserves of social capital. Social capital (S) and bought goods (x) would be complementary goods, in the sense that an increase in S implies an increase in the marginal utility of x. All this means, e.g., that I will enjoy wearing a tie more or buying a new car if my friends have done the same. This could have some implications for the influence of social networks on trust. On the one hand, it could suggest social pressure from my social network in favor of trusting behavior. That is, the potential gains of trust would be increased by the positive social sanction of trusting behavior. On the other hand, the demand for certain goods could be increased by an increase in the demand for those goods by other members of the social network. This could also increase the potential gains of trust in the case of the object of trust being those goods.
6. For example, see *El Príncipe* (Madrid: Alianza Editorial, 1992: 85, 91–92), and the *Discursos sobre la primera década de Tito Livio* (Madrid: Alianza Editorial, 1996: 70–71, 217).
7. I have taken most of the references to Vietnamese peasant communities and the activities of political entrepreneurs from Samuel Popkin's (1979) *The Rational Peasant. The Political Economy of Rural Society in Vietnam*. Los Angeles: University of California Press.

Chapter Six   The Creation of Social Trust—the Role of the State

1. Examples include a number of Scandinavian authors. Per Selle (1999), e.g., argues that, at least in the 1930s, State social policies in Norway strongly favored the creation of voluntary associations. Martii Siisiäen (1999) suggests something similar occurred in Finland. Beyond Scandinavia, some studies, such as that of Wai Fung Lam (1997: 38) on the development of irrigation associations in Taiwan, emphasize the State's role in promoting coordination between associations, reducing transaction costs and creating new associations.

2. Some references to Tocqueville in the social capital school are rather misleading. It is doubtful whether Tocqueville believed that the State was inimical to associationism. His idea was that associations can take on some of the functions that a small State, of the type existing in America in the 1830s, was performing badly (Whittington, 1998: 22–23). In my opinion, another erroneous interpretation of Tocqueville is the invocation of the French author as a precursor to Putnam's thesis about the beneficial effects of associations on democratic government. In fact, Tocqueville did not think that good government was a characteristic feature of American society. He considered that the quality of American governors was poor. The same equality that fostered participation in associations of American citizens expelled the most distinguished men from that "nasty mass politics" (Tocqueville, 1995: 185–188). The beneficial effect of participation in associations was the creation of active citizens and, in consequence, good entrepreneurs (Holmes, 1993: 34).

3. Greely e.g. (1997: 592–593), among others, considers that church attendance, and more generally membership of a religious faith, has desirable social and moral effects.

4. E. O. Wright himself (1988) uses the term "new middle class" in reference to these eight "contradictory positions within the relations of exploitation" or "contradictory positions within class relations."

5. Such views are not only defended by Conservatives. Part of the revival of the idea of "civil society" in the 1970s was the work of leftist French intellectuals, who considered that the administrative intervention of the capitalist Welfare State undermined all autonomous forms of social solidarity (Cohen and Arato, 1995: 37).

6. As noted earlier, other proponents of associative democracy attribute a positive role to the State in promoting participation in associations. For example, Joshua Cohen and Joel Rogers's proposal. They defend the active participation of the State, through the mechanisms of modern Welfare States, in fostering participation in associations by members of all social groups, and especially the least well-off (Cohen and Rogers, 1995a,b).

7. In some countries, the State subsidizes (through tax reductions) the citizen's participation in certain associations, such as unions.

8. In this section, I have shown how high levels of public expenditure, far from having a crowding-out effect on participation in associations, can foster participation. However, the observed increase in public expenditure and the parallel increase in associational density can be explained in a different way. For example, Ferejohn (1999) argues that, if the State offers citizens more information, they, in exchange for an increase in their capacity to monitor governmental action, will confer more resources to the State. Therefore, governments that are more sensitive to the monitoring of citizens will lead to States with more resources. Moreover, in accordance with social capital literature, or at least with Putnam (1993a), as well as with the arguments with scholars well removed from the social capital research paradigm, such as Rosenstone and Hansen (1993), the greater the associational density, the greater the citizen's information and, therefore, the greater the accountability of governments. If associations are promoted by the State to this end, the result, if Ferejohn's argument is correct, could be more resources for the State.

9. The size of place of residence is one of the most important variables in the social capital literature on participation in associations. Putnam includes it in his analysis of participation in associations in America in the nineteenth and early twentieth century (Putnam and Gamm, 1999). The tendency to think that "small is beautiful" has been criticized by Skocpol et al. (2000), who demonstrates that, actually, big cities were home to most of the associations created during this period.

10. I wish to thank Henar Criado for this idea.

11. According to Erik Olin Wright (1997), the propertied classes (capitalists and small employers) practice capitalist exploitation, based upon an unequal distribution of the means of production. The "new middle class" would be exploited in a capitalist sense because they do not own the

means of production, albeit less so than the working class. At the same time, however, many of the class positions included within the new middle class exert domination over the working class, as a result of their positions of authority in the workplace.

Chapter Seven   The "Virtuous Circle" of the Creation of Social Capital

1. All the references to Luco dei Marsi and Trasacco's parallel stories are taken from Caroline White's *Patrons and Partisans. A Study of Politics in Two Italian Comuni*, Cambridge: Cambridge University Press (1980).

2. That is, they would prefer to cooperate had the other done the same (or a number of them), but if none of them (or a number below a certain threshold) cooperated, he would prefer to reciprocate.

3. The social capital literature commonly distinguishes between different types of associations. Associations are distinguished by their inclusive or exclusive character (Putnam, 2000: 22; Eastis, 1998), by the heterogeneity or homogeneity of their members (Stolle and Rochon, 1998), or by their horizontal or vertical character (Putnam, 1993a). At least once, associations have been distinguished by whether or not they seek public or private goods. Boix and Posner (1996) distinguish between public-good- and private-good associations, arguing that the former create more robust social capital. I have used Boix and Posner's distinction for other purposes in this chapter.

4. A social dilemma is a situation in which private interest is in contradiction with collective interests, in which all or most people in a group act in accordance with their private interests and obtain a worse outcome than if they had ignored them (Van Lange et al., 1992: 3–4).

5. If we have more than two players, the natural generalization of tit-for-tat would be: "cooperate in the first round and keep on cooperating in successive rounds if and only if at least n players have decided to cooperate in the previous round" (Taylor, 1987, 85). For cooperation to be maintained, it is necessary that $n = N - 1$ (N being the total number of players). That is, unanimity is required (along with, of course, a sufficiently high discount rate). If $n < N - 1$, cooperation is not an equilibrium, because there are strong incentives for noncooperation in all the rounds of the game: if one of the players decides not to cooperate, the others will carry on cooperating, and the noncooperator will obtain maximum payoff in all rounds of the super-game. For this reason, none of the players will have an incentive to adopt strategies of conditional cooperation (Taylor, 1987: 86–87; Elster, 1991: 60).

Bibliography

Arrow, Kenneth J. 1974. *The Limits of Organization*. New York-Londres: W. W. Norton & Company.

Axelrod, Robert. 1984. *The Evolution of Cooperation*. New York: Basic Books.

Bacharach, Michael and Diego Gambetta. 2001. "Trust in Signs," in ed. Karen S. Cook. *Trust in Society*. New York: Russell Sage Foundation.

Becker, Gary S. and Kevin M. Murphy. 2000. *Social Economics. Market Behavior in a Social Environment*. Cambridge: Harvard University Press.

Berman, Sheri. 1997. "Civil Society and Political Institutionalization." *American Behavioral Scientist* 40 (5): 562–574.

Blackburn, Simon. 1998. "Trust, Cooperation, and Human Psychology," in ed. Valerie Braithwaite and Margaret Levi. *Trust and Governance*. New York: Russell Sage Foundation.

Blau, Peter M. 1964. *Exchange and Power in Social Life*. New York: Wiley.

Blau, Peter M. 1977. "A Macrosociological Theory of Social Structure." *American Journal of Sociology* 83 (1): 26–54.

Boix, Carles and Daniel Posner. 1996. "Making Social Capital Work: A Review of Robert Putnam's Making Democracy Work: Civic Traditions in Modern Italy." *Harvard University Centre for International Affairs Working Paper Series* 96 (4).

Booth, John A. and Patricia Richard. 1998. "Civil Society and Political Context in Central America." *American Behavioral Scientist* 42 (1): 33–46.

Bourdieu, Pierre. 1985. "The Forms of Capital," in ed. J. G. Richardson. *Handbook of Theory and Research for the Sociology of Education*. New York: Greenwood.

Bowles, Samuel and Herbert Gintis. 1990. "Contested Exchange: New Microfoundations for the Political Economy of Capitalism." *Politics and Society* 18 (2): 165–222.

Brehm, John and Wendy Rahn. 1997. "Individual-Level Evidence For the Causes and Consequences of Social Capital." *American Journal of Political Science* 41 (3): 999–1023.

Brucker, Gene. 1999. "Civic Traditions in Premodern Italy." *Journal of Interdisciplinary History* 29 (3): 357–377.

Bukharin, Nikolai. 1974. *Teoría del materialismo histórico*. Madrid: Siglo XXI.

Bullock, Allan. 1998. *Hitler and Stalin. Parallel Lives*. London: Fontana Press.

Burt, Ronald S. and Marc Knez. 1995. "Kinds of Third-Party Effects on Trust." *Rationality and Society* 7 (3): 255–292.

Buskens, Vincent and Jeroen Weesie. 2000. "An Experiment on the Effects of Embeddedness in Trust Situations. Buying a Used Car." *Rationality and Society* 12 (2): 227–253.

Calvert, Randall L. 1985. "The Value of Biased Information: A Rational Choice Model of Political Advice." *Journal of Politics* 47: 530–555.

Chamberlain, William H. 1956. "The Stalin Era and Stalin's Heirs." *Russian Review* 15 (4): 237–244.

Cicero. 2000. *Bruto [Brutus]*. Madrid: Alianza Editorial. Translator: Manuel Mañas.

Cicero. 2001. *Sobre los deberes [De Officiis]*. Madrid: Alianza Editorial. Translator: José Guillén Cabañero.

Cohen, Jean L. and Andrew Arato. 1995. *Civil Society and Political Theory*. Cambridge: The MIT Press.

Cohen, Joshua and Joel Rogers. 1995a. "Secondary Associations and Democratic Governance," in ed. Erik Olin Wright. *Associations and Democracy*. Londres: Verso.

Cohen, Joshua and Joel Rogers. 1995b. "Solidarity, Democracy, Association," in ed. Erik Olin Wright. *Associations and Democracy*. Londres: Verso.

Cohn Jr., Samuel K. 1994. "La Storia Secondo Robert Putnam." *Polis* 8 (2): 315–324.

Coleman, James S. 1988. "Social Capital in the Creation of Human Capital." *American Journal of Sociology* 94: 95–120.

Coleman, James S. 1990. *Foundations of Social Theory*. Cambridge: Harvard University Press.

Conquest, Robert. 1986. *The Harvest of Sorrow. Soviet Collectivization and the Terror-Famine*. New York: Oxford University Press.

Conquest, Robert. 1990. *The Great Terror. A Reassessment*. London: Pimlico.

Dahl, Robert. 1985. *A Preface to Economic Democracy*. Cambridge: Polity Press.

Dasgupta, Partha. 1988. "Trust as a Commodity," in ed. Diego Gambetta. *Trust*. Oxford: Basil Blackwell.

Davies, Sarah. 1997. *Popular Opinion in Stalin's Russia. Terror, Propaganda and Dissent, 1934–1941*. Cambridge: Cambridge University Press.

De Tocqueville, Alexis. 1996. *La democracia en América*. Madrid: Alianza Editorial.

Deutscher, Isaac. 1984. *Stalin. A Political Biography*. London: Penguin.

Domènech, Antoni. 1989. *De la ética a la política*. Barcelona: Crítica.

Dunn, John. 1993. "Trust," in ed. Robert E. Goodin and Philip Pettit. *A Companion to Contemporary Political Philosophy*. Londres: Blackwell.

Eastis, Carla M. 1998. "Organizational Diversity and the Production of Social Capital." *American Behavioral Scientist* 42 (1): 66–77.

Elster, Jon. 1983. *Uvas amargas*. Barcelona: Península.

Elster, Jon. 1985. *Making Sense of Marx*. Cambridge: Cambridge University Press.

Elster, Jon. 1987. "The Market and the Forum: Three Varieties of Political Theory," in ed. Jon Elster and Aanund Hylland. *Foundations of Social Choice Theory*. Cambridge: Cambridge University Press.

Elster, Jon. 1991. *El cemento de la sociedad*. Barcelona: Gedisa.

Elster, Jon. 1993a. *Political Psychology*. Cambridge: Cambridge University Press.

Elster, Jon. 1993b. "Constitution Making in Eastern Europe: Rebuilding the Boat in the Open Sea," *Public Administration* 71 (1/2): 169–217.

Elster, Jon. 1995. "Forces and Mechanisms in the Constitution-Making Process." *Duke Law Review* 45: 364–396.

Emerson, Richard M. 1962. "Power-Dependence Relations." *American Sociological Review* 27: 31–41.

Esping-Andersen, Gösta. 1993. *Los tres mundos del Estado del bienestar*. Valencia: Alfons el Magnànim.

Fearon, James D. 1998. "Deliberation as Discussion," in ed. Jon Elster. *Deliberative Democracy*. Cambridge: Cambridge University Press.

Ferejohn, John. 1999. "Accountability and Authority: Toward a Theory of Political Accountability," in ed. Adam Przeworski, Susan C. Stokes, and Bernard Manin. *Democracy, Accountability and Representation*. Cambridge: Cambridge University Press.

Figes, Orlando. 2000. *La Revolución rusa. 1891–1924*. Barcelona: Edhasa.

Fishkin, James S. and Robert C. Luskin. 2000. "The Quest for Deliberative Democracy," in ed. Michael Saward. *Democratic Innovation. Deliberation, Representation and Association*. Londres: Routledge.

Foley, Michael W. and Bob Edwards. 1998a. "Beyond Tocqueville: Civil Society and Social Capital in Comparative Perspective." *American Behavioral Scientist* 42 (1): 5–20.

Foley, Michael W. and Bob Edwards. 1998b. "Civil Society and Social Capital Beyond Putnam." *American Behavioral Scientist* 42 (1): 124–139.

Foley, Michael W. and Bob Edwards. 1999. "Is it Time to Disinvest in Social Capital?" *Journal of Public Policy* 19 (2): 141–173.

Fung Lam, Wai. 1997. "Institutional Design of Public Agencies and Coproduction: A Study of Irrigation Associations in Taiwan," in ed. Peter Evans. *State and Society Sinergy. Government and Social Capital in Development.* Berkeley: University of Berkeley Press.

Funk, Carolyne. 1998. "Practicing What We Preach? The Influence of a Societal Interest Value on Civic Engagement." *Political Psychology* 19 (3): 601–614.

Gambetta, Diego. 1988a. "Can We Trust Trust?" in ed. Diego Gambetta. *Trust.* Oxford: Basil Blackwell.

Gambetta, Diego. 1988b. "Mafia: The Price of Distrust," in ed. Diego Gambetta. *Trust.* Oxford: Basil Blackwell.

Gambetta, Diego. 1998. "Claro!: An Essay on Discursive Machismo," in ed. Jon Elster. *Deliberative Democracy.* Cambridge: Cambridge University Press.

Gamm, Gerarld and Robert D. Putnam. 1999. "The Growth of Voluntary Associations in America, 1840–1940." *Journal of Interdisciplinary History* 29 (3): 511–557.

Gautschi, Thomas. 2000. "History Effects in Social Dilemma Situations." *Rationality and Society* 12 (2): 131–162.

Genicot, Léopold. 1993. *Comunidades rurales en el Occidente medieval.* Barcelona: Crítica.

Getty, J. Arch and Naumov, Oleg. 1999. *The Road to Terror. Stalin and the Self-Destruction of Bolsheviks 1932–1939.* London: Yale University Press.

Goodin, Robert E. 2000. "Trusting Individuals Versus Trusting Institutions. Generalizing the Case of Contract." *Rationality and Society* 12 (4): 381–395.

Granovetter, Mark. 1974. "The Strength of Weak Ties." *American Journal of Sociology* 78 (6): 1360–1380.

Granovetter, Mark. 1985. "Economic Action and Social Structure: The Problem of Embeddedness." *American Journal of Sociology* 91 (3): 481–510.

Greely, Andrew. 1997. "Coleman Revisited. Religous Structures as a Source of Social Capital." *American Behavioral Scientist* 40 (5): 587–594.

Green, Melanie and Timothy Brock. 1998. "Trust, Mood, and Outcomes of Friendship Determine Preferences for Real Versus Ersatz Social Capital." *Political Psychology* 19 (3): 527–544.

Greif, Avner. 1989. *The Organization of Long-Distance Trade: Reputation and Coalitions in the "Geniza" Documents and Genoa During the Eleventh and the Twelfth Centuries,* Ph. D. dissertation. Ann Arbor, Michigan: UNI Dissertation Services.

Hall, Peter. 1999. "Social Capital in Britain." *British Journal of Political Science* 29: 417–461.

Hansen, Mogens Heman. 1999. *The Athenian Democracy in the Age of Demosthenes.* Londres: University of Oklahoma Press.

Hardin, Garrett. 1978. "Political Requirements for Preserving Our Common Heritage," in ed. H. P. Bokaw. *Wildlife and America.* Washington DC: Council on Environmental Quality.

Hardin, Russell. 1993. "The Street-Level Epistemology of Trust." *Politics and Society* 21 (4): 505–529.

Hardin, Russell. 1995. *One for All. The Logic of Group Conflict.* Princeton: Princeton University Press.

Hardin, Russell. 1996. "Trustworthiness." *Ethics* 107 (1): 26–42.

Hardin, Russell. 2001. "Conceptions and Explanations of Trust," in ed. Karen Cook. *Trust in Society.* New York: Russell Sage.

Hardin, Russell. 2002. *Trust and Trustworthiness.* New York: Russell Sage.

Hargreaves, Shaun P. and Yanis Varoufakis. 1995. *Game Theory. A Critical Introduction*. Londres: Routledge.

Hawthorn, Geoffrey. 1988. "Three Ironies in Trust," in ed. Diego Gambetta. *Trust*. Oxford: Basil Blackwell.

Hayashi, Nahoko, Elinor Ostrom, James Walker and Toshio Yamagishi. 1999. "Reciprocity, Trust and the Sense of Control." *Rationality and Society* 11 (1): 27–46.

Heilbroner, R. L. 1974. *An Inquiry into the Human Prospect*. New York: Norton.

Heimer, Carol A. 2001. "Solving the Problem of Trust," in ed. Karen S. Cook. *Trust in Society*. New York: Russell Sage Foundation.

Herreros, Francisco. 2003. "The Dilemma of Social Democracy in 1914: Chauvinism or Social Dilemma?" *Rationality and Society* 15 (3): 325–344.

Herreros, Francisco and Henar Criado. 2003. "In Whom We Trust? The Creation of Particularised Trust Inside Associations." *European Political Science* 2 (3): 56–61.

Hirst, Paul. 1994. *Associative Democracy*. Cambridge: Polity Press.

Hobbes, Thomas. 1992. *Leviathan*. Madrid: Alianza Editorial.

Hollis, Martin. 1998. *Trust Within Reason*. Cambridge: Cambridge University Press.

Holmes, Stephen. 1993. "Tocqueville and Democracy," in ed. David Copp, Jean Hampton, and John Roemer. *The Idea of Democracy*. Cambridge: Cambridge University Press.

Jansen, Marc and Nikita Petrov. 2002. *Stalin's Loyal Executioner: People's Commissar Nikolai Ezhov, 1895–1940*. Stanford: Hoover Institution Press.

Jones, Karen. 1996. "Trust as an Affective Attitude." *Ethics* 107 (1): 4–25.

Jones, Kelvyn and Nina Bullen. 1994. "People and Places: The Multilevel Model as a General Framework for the Quantitative Análisis of Geographical Data." *Economic Geography* 70: 252–272.

Kenworthy, L. 1997. "Civic Engagement, Social Capital, and Economic Cooperation." *American Behavioral Scientist* 40 (5): 645–656.

Kershaw, Ian. 2000. *Hitler. 1936–1945*. Barcelona: Península.

Kirby, David. 1986. *War, Peace and Revolution. International Socialism at the Crossroads 1914–1918*. Hants: Gower House.

Knight, Amy. 1993. *Beria. Stalin's First Lieutenant*. Princeton: Princeton University Press.

Kolankiewicz, George. 1996. "Social Capital and Social Change." *British Journal of Sociology* 47 (3): 427–441.

Kreps, David. 1990. "Corporate Culture and Economic Theory," in ed. James Alt and Kenneth Shepsle. *Perspectives on Positive Political Economy*. Cambridge: Cambridge University Press.

Kreutz, Barbara. 1996. *Before the Normans. Southern Italy in the Ninth and Tenth Centuries*. Philadelphia: University of Pennsylvania Press.

Kriegel, Annie. 1985. "La Segunda Internacional (1889–1914)," in ed. J. Droz, M. Rebérioux, P. Guichonnet, P. Vilar, F. Bédarida, R. Portal, M. Debouzy, J. Chesneaux, and A. Kriegel. *Historia general del socialismo. De 1875 a 1918*. Barcelona: Destino.

Kriegel, Annie and Jean-Jacques Becker. 1964. *1914. La guerre et le mouvement ouvrier français*. Paris: Armand Colin.

Kydd, Andrew. 2000. "Overcoming Mistrust." *Rationality and Society* 12 (4): 397–424.

Lahno, Bernd. 1995. "Trust and Strategic Rationality." *Rationality and Society* 7 (4): 442–464.

Lange, Peter. 1991. "Sindicatos, trabajadores y reglamentación salarial: bases racionales para el acuerdo," in ed. John H. Goldthorpe. *Orden y conflicto en el capitalismo contemporáneo*. Madrid: Ministerio de Trabajo y Seguridad Social.

Leibenstein, Harvey. 1987. "On Some Economic Aspects of a Fragile Input: Trust," in ed. George R. Feiwel. *Arrow and the Foundations of the Theory of Economic Policy*. New York: New York University Press.

Lenin, V. I. 1974. *El imperialismo. Fase superior del capitalismo*. Madrid: Fundamentos.

Lenin, V. I. 1980. "El imperialismo y la escisión del socialismo," in V. I. Lenin. *Marx, Engels, marxismo*. Pekín: Ediciones en Lenguas Extranjeras.

Levi, Margaret. 1993. "Review of *Making Democracy Work*." *Comparative Political Studies* 26 (3): 375–379.

Levi, Margaret. 1996a. "Social and Unsocial Capital: A Review Essay of Robert Putnam's *Making Democracy Work*." *Politics and Society* 24 (1): 45–55.

Levi, Margaret. 1996b. "A State of Trust." Florence: European University Institute Working Paper 96/23.

Levi, Margaret. 1997. *Consent, Dissent and Patriotism*. Cambridge: Cambridge University Press.

Lin, Nan. 2001. *Social Capital. A Theory of Social Structure and Action*. Cambridge: Cambridge University Press.

Locke, John. 1998. *An Essay Concerning Human Understanding*. Kent: Wordsworth.

Loury, G. 1977. "A Dynamic Theory of Racial Income Differences," in eds. P. A. Wallace and A. Le Mund, *Women, Minorities, and Employment Discrimination*. Lexington: Lexington Books.

Luhmann, Niklas. 1979. *Trust and Power*. New York: John Wiley and Sons.

Machiavelli, Nicolás. 1992. *El Príncipe*. Madrid: Alianza Editorial.

Machiavelli, Nicolás. 1996. *Discursos sobre la primera década de Tito Livio*. Madrid: Alianza Editorial.

Mandel, Ernest. 1978. *Sobre la historia del movimiento obrero*. Barcelona: Fontamara.

Mansbridge, Jane. 1999. "Altruistic Trust," in ed. Mark E. Warren. *Democracy and Trust*. Cambridge: Cambridge University Press.

Maravall, José María. 1999. "Accountability and Manipulation," in ed. Adam Przeworski, Susan C. Stokes, and Bernard Manin. *Democracy, Accountability and Representation*. Cambridge: Cambridge University Press.

Maynard Smith, John. 1982. *Evolution and the Theory of Games*. Cambridge: Cambridge University Press.

Messick, David M. and Roderick M. Kramer. 2001. "Trust as a Form of Sallow Morality," in ed. Karen S. Cook. *Trust in Society*. New York: Russell Sage.

Miller, Gary J. 1992. *Managerial Dilemmas*. Cambridge: Cambridge University Press.

Miller, Gary. 2001. "Why is Trust Necessary in Organizations? The Moral Hazard of Profit Maximization," in ed. Karen S. Cook. *Trust in Society*. New York: Russell Sage Foundation.

Minkoff, Debra C. 1997. "Producing Social Capital. National Social Movements and Civic Society." *American Behavioral Scientist* 40 (5): 606–619.

Mondak, Jeffrey and Adam F. Gearing. 1998. "Civic Engagement in a Post-Communist State." *Political Psychology* 19 (3): 615–637.

Molm, Linda D. 1997. *Coercive Power in Social Exchange*. Cambridge: Cambridge University Press.

Morlino, Leonardo. 1995. "Italy's Civic Divide." *Journal of Democracy* 6 (1): 173–177.

Newton, Kenneth. 1997. "Social Capital and Democracy." *American Behavioral Scientist* 40 (5): 575–586.

Newton, Kenneth. 1999a. "Social Capital and Democracy in Modern Europe," in ed. Jan W. Van Deth, Marco Maraffi, Ken Newton, and Paul F. Whiteley. *Social Capital and European Democracy*. London: Routledge.

Newton, Kenneth. 1999b. "Social and Political Trust in Established Democracies," in ed. Pippa Norris. *Critical Citizens. Global Support for Democratic Governance*. Oxford: Oxford University Press.

Nichols, Thomas M. 1996. "Russian Democracy and Social Capital." *Social Science Information* 35 (4): 629–642.

North, Douglass C. 1990. *Institutions, Institutional Change and Economic Performance*. Cambridge: Cambridge University Press.

Nowland-Foreman, Garth. 1998. "Purchase-of-Service Contracting, Voluntary Organizations, and Civil Society. Dissecting the Goose That Lays the Golden Eggs?" *American Behavioral Scientist* 42 (1): 108–123.

Offe, Claus. 1999. "How Can We Trust Our Fellow Citizens?" in ed. Mark E. Warren. *Democracy and Trust*. Cambridge: Cambridge University Press.

Olson, Mancur. 1973. *The Logic of Collective Action. Public Goods and the Theory of Groups*. Cambridge: Harvard University Press.

O'Neill, Claire. 1996. "Making Democracy Work: Putnam and His Critics." *South European Society and Politics* 1 (2): 307–318.

Ostrom, Elinor. 1990. *Governing the Commons. The Evolution of Institutions for Collective Action*. Cambridge: Cambridge University Press.

Ostrom, Elinor, Roy Gardner, and James Walker. 1994. *Rules, Games and Common-Pool Resources*. Michigan: The University of Michigan Press.

Padgen, Anthony. 1988. "The Destruction of Trust and Its Economic Consequences in the Case of Eighteenth-Century Naples," in ed. Diego Gambetta. *Trust*. Londres: Basil Blackwell.

Pettit, Philip. 1995. "The Cunning of Trust." *Philosophy and Public Affairs* 24 (3): 202–225.

Pharr, Susan J., Robert D. Putnam, and Russell J. Dalton. 2000. "A Quarter-Century of Declining Confidence." *Journal of Democracy* 11 (2): 5–25.

Pierson, Paul. 1996. "The New Politics of the Welfare State." *World Politics* 48: 143–179.

Popkin, Samuel L. 1979. *The Rational Peasant. The Political Economy of Rural Society*. Los Angeles: The University of California Press.

Popkin, Samuel L. 1991. *The Reasoning Voter. Communication and Persuasion in Presidential Campaigns*. Chicago: The University of Chicago Press.

Putnam, Robert D. 1993a. *Making Democracy Work. Civic Traditions in Modern Italy*. Princeton: Princeton University Press.

Putnam, Robert. 1993b. "The Prosperous Community. Social Capital and Public Life." *The American Prospect* 13: 35–42.

Putnam, Robert D. 2000. *Bowling Alone. The Collapse and Revival of American Community*. New York: Simon and Schuster.

Putnam, Robert D. and Gerald Gamm. 1999. "The Growth of Voluntary Associations in America, 1840–1940." *Journal of Interdisciplinary History* 29 (4): 511–557.

Rasmusen, Eric. 1989. *Games and Information*. Cambridge: Blackwell.

Rawls, John. 1995. "The Domain of the Political and Overlapping Consensus," in ed. John E. Roemer, Jean Hampton, and David Copp. *The Idea of Democracy*. Cambridge: Cambridge University Press.

Rebérioux, Madeleine. 1985. "El socialismo y la primera guerra mundial (1914–1918)," in J. Droz, M. Rebérioux, P. Guichonnet, P. Vilar, R. Portal, M. Debouzy, J. Chesnaux, and A. Kriegel. *Historia general del socialismo. De 1875 a 1918*. Barcelona: Ediciones Destino.

Reynolds, Susan. 1997. *Kingdoms and Communities in Western Europe*. Oxford: Oxford University Press.

Rosenstone, Steven and Mark Hansen. 1993. *Mobilization, Participation and Democracy in America*. New York: Macmillan.

Rousseau, Jean Jacques. 1990. *Discurso sobre el origen y los fundamentos de la desigualdad entre los hombres*. Madrid: Tecnos.

Sabetti, Filippo. 1996. "Path Dependency and Civic Culture: Some Lessons From Italy About Interpreting Social Experiments." *Politics and Society* 24 (1): 19–44.

Sandefour, Rebecca L. and Edward O. Laumann. 1998. "A Paradigm for Social Capital." *Rationality and Society* 10 (4): 481–501.

Sasson, Donald. 1997. *One Hundred Years of Socialism. The West European Left in the Twentieth Century*. Londres: Fontana Press.

Seligman, Adam B. 1997. *The Problem of Trust*. Princeton: Princeton University Press.

Selle, Per. 1999. "The Transformation of the Voluntary Sector in Norway. A Decline in Social Capital?" in ed. Jan Van Deth, Marco Maraffi, Ken Newton, and Paul F. Whiteley. *Social Capital and European Democracy*. Londres: Routledge.

Service, Robert. 1997. *A History of Twentieth-Century Russia*. Cambridge: Harvard University Press.

Shah, Dhavan V. 1998. "Civic Engagement, Interpersonal Trust, and Television Use: An Individual-Level Assesment of Social Capital." *Political Psychology* 19 (3): 469–496.

Siisiäinen, Martti. 1999. "Voluntary Associations and Social Capital in Finland," in ed. Jan Van Deth, Marco Maraffi, Ken Newton, and Paul F. Whiteley. *Social Capital and European Democracy*. Londres: Routledge.

Skocpol, Theda. 1996. "Unraveling from Above." *The American Prospect* 25: 20–25.

Skocpol, Theda. 1997. "The Tocqueville Problem." *Social Science History* 21 (4): 455–479.

Skocpol, Theda, Marshall Ganz, and Ziad Munson. 2000. "A Nation of Organizers: The Institutional Origins of Civic Voluntarism in the United States." *American Political Science Review* 94 (3): 527–546.

Stolle, Dietlind. 1998. "Bowling Together, Bowling Alone: The Development of Generalized Trust in Voluntary Associations." *Political Psychology* 19 (3): 497–525.

Stolle, Dietlind. 2000. "Social Capital—A New Research Agenda? Toward an Attitudinal Approach," paper presented in the workshop about "Social Capital and Voluntary Associations," ECPR Joint Sessions, Copenhague.

Stolle, Dietlind and Thomas R. Rochon. 1998. "Are all Asociations Alike? Member Diversity, Associational Type and the Creation of Social Capital." *American Behavioral Scientists* 42 (1): 47–65.

Stolle, Dietlind and Thomas R. Rochon. 1999. "The Myth of American Exceptionalism. A Three-Nation Comparison of Associational Membership and Social Capital," in ed. Jan Van Deth, Marco Maraffi, Ken Newton, and Paul F. Whiteley. *Social Capital and European Democracy*. Londres: Routledge.

Sunstein, Cass R. 1988. "Beyond the Republican Revival." *Yale Law Journal* 97: 1539–1590.

Sztompka, Piotr. 1999. *Trust. A Sociological Theory*. Cambridge: Cambridge University Press.

Tarrow, Sidney. 1996. "Making Social Science Work Across Space and Time: A Critical Reflection on Robert Putnam's *Making Democracy Work*." *American Political Science Review* 90 (2): 389–397.

Taylor, A. J. P. 1971. *The Struggle for Mastery in Europe. 1848–1918*. Oxford: Oxford University Press.

Taylor, Michael. 1987. *The Possibility of Cooperation*. Cambridge: Cambridge University Press.

Taylor, Michael. 1988. "Revolutionary Collective Action," in ed. Michael Taylor. *Rationality and Revolution*. Cambridge: Cambridge University Press.

Taylor, Michael. 1996. "Good Government: On Hierarchy, Social Capital and the Limitations of Rational Choice Theory." *The Journal of Political Philosophy* 4 (1): 1–28.

Thompson, E. P. 1989. *La formación de la clase obrera en Inglaterra*. Barcelona: Crítica.

Tucker, Robert C. 1990. *Stalin in Power. The Revolution from Above, 1928–1941*. New York and London: Norton.

Tversky, Amos and Daniel Kahneman. 1986. "Beliefs in the Law of Small Numbers," in ed. Daniel Kahneman, Paul Slovic, and Amos Tversky. *Judgement Under Uncertainty: Heuristics and Biases*. Cambridge: Cambridge University Press.

Uslaner, Eric M. 1999a. "Democracy and Social Capital," in ed. Mark E. Warren. *Democracy and Trust*. Cambridge: Cambridge University Press.

Uslaner, Eric M. 1999b. "Morality Plays. Social Capital and Moral Behaviour in Anglo-American Democracies," in ed. Jan Van Deth, Marco Maraffi, Ken Newton, and Paul F. Whiteley. *Social Capital and European Democracy*. Londres: Routledge.

Valelly, Richard M. 1996. "Couch-Potato Democracy?" *The American Prospect* 25: 25–26.

Van Lange, Paul A., Wim Liebrand, David Messick, and Henk Wilke. 1992. "Introduction and Literature Review," in ed. Liebrand, Messick, and Wilke. *Social Dilemmas. Theoretical Issues and Research Findings*. Oxford: Pergamon Press.

Verba, Sidney, Kay Schlozman, and Henry Brady. 1995. *Voice and Equality. Civic Voluntarism in American Politics*. Cambridge: Harvard University Press.

Verba, Sidney, Norman H. Nie, and Jae-on Kim. 1978. *Participation and Political Equality*. Cambridge: Cambridge University Press.

White, Caroline. 1980. *Patrons and Partisans. A Study of Politics in Two Southern Italian Comuni*. Cambridge: Cambridge University Press.

Whiteley, Paul F. 1999. "The Origins of Social Capital," in ed. Jan W. Van Deth, Marco Maraffi, Ken Newton, and Paul F. Whiteley. *Social Capital and European Democracy*. Londres: Routledge.

Whittington, Keith E. 1998. "Revisiting Tocqueville's America." *American Behavioral Scientist* 42 (1): 21–32.

Wielers, Rudi. 1997. "The Wages of Trust. The Case of Child Minders." *Rationality and Society* 9 (3): 351–371.

Williamson, Oliver E. 1985. *The Economic Institutions of Capitalism*. New York: The Free Press.

Woodside, Alexander B. 1976. *Community and Revolution in Modern Vietnam*. Boston: Houghton Mifflin Company.

Wright, Erik Olin. 1988. "Qué tiene de media la clase media?" in comp. John E. Roemer. *El marxismo: una perspectiva analítica*. México: Fondo de Cultura Económica.

Wright, Erik Olin. 1997. *Class Counts. Comparative Studies in Class Analysis*. Cambridge: Cambridge University Press.

Yamagishi, Toshio. 2001. "Trust as a Form of Social Intelligence," in ed. Karen Cook. *Trust in Society*. New York: Russell Sage Foundation.

Yamagishi, Toshio, Karen S. Cook, and Motoki Watabe. 1998. "Uncertainty, Trust and Commitment Formation in the United States and Japan." *American Journal of Sociology* 104 (1): 165–194.

INDEX

sociological analysis of, 3
systems of, 6, 28, 48, 105, 132 n.2 Ch. 2
Trustworthiness, 7, 8, 9, 12, 13, 22, 29, 44,
  56, 58, 65, 76, 77
  and civic virtue, 17–18
  and cooperation, 10
  and information, 30, 47, 74–75, 123
  and participation in associations, 28,
    52, 53–54, 61, 109
  and reputation, 11, 12, 22, 44, 45
  and sanctions, 33–36
  and self-esteem, 46–47
  and signals, 51, 53, 64, 69, 70, 71, 75
Tucker, Robert, 37
Tuscany: and the Spanish rule, 25
Tversky, Amos, 53

Under and Supra socialized conceptions
  of the human being, 3, 19
United Kingdom, 79, 80, 87, 88, 91, 111
United States, 79, 80, 84, 87, 88, 91, 94,
  96, 97
  and the New Deal, 85
Uslaner, Eric, 8, 28

Vallely, Richard M., 72
Values, 102
  and the definition of social capital, 6,
    17, 123

collectivist, 108
Van Lange, Paul A., 135 n. 4 Ch. 7
Varoufakis, Yanis, 116
Versailles Treaty, 28
Vertical relations, 103, 104
Verba, Sidney, 86
Vienna, 29
Vietnam, 66, 67, 68, 69, 70,
  71, 124
Vietnamese Communist Party,
  69, 70

Weak ties, 15, 24
Weesie, Jeroen, 11
Welfare States, 86, 87, 88, 91, 96,
  99, 124
  conservative, 90, 94
  liberal, 90, 94
  social-democratic, 90, 94
White, Caroline, 104, 135 n. 1 Ch. 7
Whiteley, Paul, 17, 53
Whitington, Keith E., 134 n. 2 Ch. 6
Wielers, Rudi, 31
Williamson, Oliver, 52
Woodside, Alexander B., 69, 70
Wright, Erik Olin, 81, 92, 134 n. 4 Ch. 6,
  134 n. 11 Ch. 6

Yamagishi, Toshio, 8, 53, 58